First published in Ireland
2014 by Onstream,
Currabaha, Cloghroe
County Cork, Ireland.
www.onstream.ie

The moral right of the author
has been asserted. All rights reserved.
No part of this work may be reproduced
or utilised in any form by any means
electronic or mechanical, including
photocopying, recording or any
information storage and retrieval system
without prior permission
of the publishers.

Copyright © onstream
Copyright © Recipes Karen Austin
Photographs copyright
© Arna Rún Rúnarsdóttir
and Jean-Marcel Coulombeau

ISBN: 9781897685 58 7

Author
Karen Austin

Photography
Arna Rún Rúnarsdóttir

Additional photography
Jean-Marcel Coulombeau
endpapers; 2, 3, 9, 12, 19
20, 32, and pp 171, 173, 176

Editor
Roz Crowley

Sub-editor
Aisling Lyons

Book design and production
Tony O'Hanlon
Propeller, Galway

Printing
KPS Colour Print

Karen Austin

THE LETTERCOLLUM COOKBOOK

Recipes
from the Kitchen
Project

8	Our Journey
10	*Salads*
38	*Soups*
52	*Fishy Dishes*
74	*Chorizo Infiltration*
84	*Vegetarian Mains*
120	*Savoury Tarts*
134	*Sweet Things*
168	Gluten-free recipes
172	Thanks
174	Index
176	Profiles

Our journey Karen Austin

I moved to Ireland thirty years ago with my partner Con who, like many Irish emigrants, had always dreamt of returning home. I was on my way to Australia one Christmas when I visited West Cork with him. After a week of glorious blue skies, I was seduced; little did I know that this was unusual weather. Moving here was quite a turnabout and the climate had me in shock for years. It was difficult to comprehend how different it was from Kent in the south-east of England where I grew up. We got together with a group of friends and family and bought a large, rather dilapidated Victorian house with twelve acres in West Cork. The house was more large than beautiful but the run-down stable block and one-acre walled garden captured our imaginations. The house had been used as a convent in a former life and came complete with a 'chapel' and confessional. This chapel room had a big stained glass window, which we left, but the rest we set about de-institutionalising: removing the linoleum and sanding the floors back to their former glory.

The plan was to 'live the good life', get away from pollution and traffic jams and try our hands at sustainable living. We had grand plans and no experience – quite a combination.

The garden had been neglected for years and was full of couch grass, which strangled whatever we tried to grow. We were determined to grow organically, so the first couple of years were spent digging the garden to remove the couch grass and other meanies. Gradually the garden flourished. We grew anything edible that we could, and between the garden and the glasshouse we had more food than we could possibly eat. We made jam and pickles, and filled the freezer with vegetables – which we never got around to eating as there was always something more appealing ready in the garden.

We also had a herd of goats for milking who were like the resident Houdinis, forever escaping to the neighbour's field where the grass obviously looked greener. This was all hard work and good fun but it didn't pay the bills. We tried to sell our vegetables locally but they weren't uniform in size and our cucumbers weren't straight enough for the shops. Realising we couldn't eat the view, Con and I began making bread that we would deliver locally. It was popular enough, but the petrol cost of the deliveries ate up a lot of our profit so we had to put our thinking caps on again.

The next venture was more successful. At this stage the original crew had dwindled and gone off to seek fame and fortune elsewhere so for the most part we (myself, Con and our three children) had a large and rather empty house. We decided to open a hostel. Hostels were very popular in Ireland at that time and the summer months would see the house bursting at the seams. The vegetable garden was in full swing and each day we offered a three-course vegetarian dinner for a bargain price. Basically the starter was whatever we had eaten ourselves for lunch – soup, salad or hummus – and the main course, whatever we were going to have for dinner. Dessert was simple: rhubarb fool in the spring, strawberries and cream or blackcurrant mousse in the summer, and apple pies or apple and blackberry crumble in the autumn.

Over time the menu became more sophisticated and we got a reputation for serving good food. People from the locality started to come for dinner and we expanded the menu to include fish and meat. Hostels and fine dining don't really go so well together so, as the demand for private rooms grew, we decided to transform the hostel into a guesthouse.

It was a slightly Fawlty Towers affair but we had our fans and received good reviews. We made everything from scratch and on top of all the usual fare we also made fresh pasta, ice-cream and croissants – you name it, we tried our hand at it. We even kept pigs, feeding them all the scraps from the restaurant and then butchering them to make the bacon and sausages for the breakfast.

Big houses are like sponges, they just soak up money. There was always something requiring urgent attention and the rules and regulations just kept coming – especially difficult to comply with when your house is a listed property. It was hard to get ahead and each year, after an insanely busy season, we would slip a little further into debt. Eventually, fed up with working night and day and being broke, we decided to bail out. We sold the big house but kept the smaller house in the stable block and the walled vegetable garden.

This meant the pressure was off, but soon we were buried in more vegetables than we knew what to do with. This is when the Kitchen Project began. We opened our shop in Clonakilty, The Lettercollum Kitchen Project, built a kitchen at the back and began to make food using all our beautiful produce.

It was good to have a day job and it also gave us the opportunity to travel again. We did miss the creativity of putting food on plates, but this was remedied by our taking groups of Irish people to Spain and France to teach them how to cook.

These days our cooking classes are held at Lettercollum. We cook at the shop and we travel for fun, poking our noses into other people's kitchens, collecting new recipes.

This book is a collection of recipes that we enjoy eating and are not too complicated to make. It is mostly vegetarian but our weekly fish dinners have slipped in and, as we occasionally enjoy a little chorizo with our beans, a few of those recipes have sneaked in too.

We hope that you enjoy making and eating them.

Salads

Asian Slaw 12

Beetroot, Caramelised Goat's Cheese and Pumpkin Seed Salad 14

Carrot, Avocado and Wakame Salad 16

Green Bean Salad with Lemon and Parmesan 18

Jen's Broccoli Salad 20

Red Cabbage, Celeriac, Apple and Hazelnut Salad 22

Raul's Catalan Artichokes with Aioli 24

Nectarine, Pink Peppercorn and Mint Tabbouleh 26

Quinoa and Chickpea Salad 28

Puy Lentil, Pea, Feta and Mint Salad 30

Summer Chickpea and Tuna Salad 32

New Potato and Smoked Mackerel Salad 34

Som Tam 36

Asian Slaw

This salad is equally delicious summer and winter. It's a version of coleslaw with sesame and ginger dressing. Under-ripe or green mangoes are the secret ingredient to this assembly and the two different cabbages give an interesting texture.

½ red cabbage
handful mangetout peas
½ green cabbage
250g bean sprouts
1 under-ripe mango
2 tbsp sesame seeds
salt

Dressing
25ml red or white wine vinegar
1 tsp Dijon mustard
150ml sunflower or rapeseed oil
25ml toasted sesame oil
25ml soy sauce
pinch sugar (optional)
large knob fresh ginger
1–2 cloves garlic

Serves 4–6

Finely slice the red cabbage, sprinkle with a little salt, toss, and leave for about 30 minutes, then pat dry with a little kitchen roll.

Top and tail the mangetout. Bring a pot of water to the boil, add a little salt and drop in the mangetout. Count to twenty, take the mangetout out and refresh them with cold water. Drain and put aside.

Finely slice the green cabbage. Rinse the bean sprouts and drain well. Cut the mango into skinny julienne strips.

Toast the sesame seeds in a dry frying pan until they are golden and start to pop.

For the dressing, whisk the vinegar and mustard together in a small bowl, then slowly whisk in the oils and soy sauce and sugar, if using. Grate the ginger coarsely – no need to peel – then gather together in your hand and squeeze the juice into the dressing. Discard the ginger.

Mix all the vegetables and the sesame seeds. Season with a little salt and toss with the dressing.

Beetroot, Caramelised Goat's Cheese and Pumpkin Seed Salad

This recipe is an old favourite in our household. We use chèvre – French goat's cheese logs – or Irish St Tola, which is mild and creamy. This combines perfectly with the cooked beetroot and toasted pumpkin seeds in this salad. If you are lucky enough to be able to get your hands on some golden beets or striped choggia beets as well as the regular type, your salad will be all the more beautiful. Mix as much and as many of them as you can get your hands on.

500g beetroot
25g pumpkin seeds
soy sauce
1 tsp Dijon mustard
1 tbsp white balsamic vinegar
2–3 tbsp pumpkin seed oil
4–5 tbsp sunflower oil
handful chives, chopped
150g goat's cheese
2 tbsp honey
selection of salad leaves for each plate
salt and pepper

Serves 2–4

Preheat the oven to 220°C (425°F) Gas Mark 7.

Wash the beetroots under running water. Snap off the stems and put into a saucepan. Cover with water and bring to the boil. Put a lid on, turn the heat down and simmer for 20–30 minutes, depending on the size (smaller beets will be sweeter than large ones). Test with a knife and when they are tender, drain and run under a cold tap. When cool, peel and chop into small chunks.

Toast the pumpkin seeds gently in a dry frying pan until they begin to pop and become golden, then take off the heat and toss with a little soy sauce.

Put the Dijon mustard into a small bowl and whisk in the vinegar and oils. Season and toss with the beetroot and chopped chives.

Slice the goat's cheese into about half-centimetre slices and put on a baking tray with 1 tsp of honey on top of each piece. Set honey is best as runny honey has too much of a head start in escaping. Put into the hot oven and bake for 3–4 minutes, until the honey is bubbling.

Put a handful of salad leaves on each plate, add a mound of the beetroot mix and gently slide a piece of roasted goat's cheese on top. Scatter with a few pumpkin seeds and serve.

Carrot, Avocado and Wakame Salad

It seems like we have been eating this salad forever. We discovered seaweed thirty years ago when we frequented Japanese restaurants in Antwerp, Belgium, where we used to live. It became all the rage to play with seaweed in the kitchen: we cooked kombu with beans; made sushi with nori; toasted it; and crumbled it onto soups. We also made salads with wakame, which is very easy to use. It's sold dried so we keep it in the pantry and whenever we want to use it we just snip it into small pieces, pour boiling water over it and let it soak while we prepare the rest of the salad. It goes very well with cucumber but my personal favourite combination is this salad. A great home-alone dish, I often eat it for lunch as it provides a real vitality buzz in the middle of a busy day.

5g wakame seaweed
200g carrots
1 small ripe avocado
1 tbsp sunflower seeds
1 tbsp pumpkin seeds
soy sauce or tamari

Dressing
½ tsp Dijon mustard
1 dssp white balsamic vinegar
3–4 tbsp olive or rapeseed oil
soy sauce or tamari

Serves 2–4

Snip the wakame into small pieces with a pair of scissors and put it into a bowl. Pour over enough boiling water to cover.

Peel and grate the carrots and put them into a serving bowl.

Cut the avocado into quarters, remove the skin and chop the flesh into small pieces onto the carrot.

Put the sunflower seeds and pumpkin seeds into a dry frying pan and toast on medium heat until the seeds become golden (the pumpkins seeds will pop a little bit).

When the seeds are golden remove from the heat and shake a little soy sauce or tamari over them. Shake the sauce and the pan at the same time to get an even distribution.

Now for the dressing, put the Dijon mustard into a small bowl. Whisk in the vinegar with a fork, then the oil. Season with a splash of soy sauce or tamari.

Drain the wakame and give it a good shake. Put a little pile in the middle of the serving bowl, on top of the carrots and avocado, and scatter over the seeds. Just before serving, drizzle the dressing on top.

Green Bean Salad with Lemon and Parmesan

Green beans cooked until they just squeak need very little else done to them. We toss them in a little vinaigrette with lemon, red onion and Parmesan.

450g French beans
1 red onion
50g Parmesan cheese, grated
large handful basil
salt and black pepper

Dressing
1 clove garlic
1 tsp Dijon mustard
1 tbsp white balsamic or white wine vinegar
75ml olive oil
25ml sunflower oil
finely grated zest of 1 lemon

Serves 4–6

Bring a large pot of salted water to the boil. Top and tail the beans and when the water is boiling add them to the pot. Cook for about 4 minutes at full heat. Test a bean. It should squeak when you bite it, barely tender. Strain and plunge into cold water.

Peel and thinly slice the red onion and rub with a little salt. Put aside.

For the dressing, finely chop the garlic and mix with the Dijon mustard and vinegar. Using a fork, whisk in the oils. Stir in the lemon zest. Taste, and season.

Drain the green beans, snap them in half if they are bigger than bitesized, and put them in a bowl together with the red onion and grated Parmesan.

Take the basil leaves off their stalks, tear into small pieces and add to the bowl.

Toss everything together with the vinaigrette. Season with a little salt and black pepper. Serve at room temperature.

Jen's Broccoli Salad

I was given this recipe on a beach in Thailand. We were sitting around, as you do, discussing this, that, and a little bit about food with a Danish guy called Jens. He suddenly leapt up and rushed off to get a pen and paper so he could give me the recipe for the best ever raw broccoli salad – all the rage in Denmark, he said, and seriously good. I wrote his instructions down and carefully stashed the recipe to try when I got home. It is seriously good and salads are always welcome in my kitchen – they keep the antibodies alert! The original recipe is made with a salad dressing called Miracle Whip, but I've used mayonnaise, red wine vinegar and sour cream instead. It tastes good. The original salad was also topped with a scattering of crispy bacon bits which are a good addition if you fancy.

1 handful pine nuts
1 handful raisins
1 medium red onion
1 head broccoli

Dressing
1 egg yolk
1 tsp Dijon mustard
200ml rapeseed or sunflower oil
50ml olive oil
1 tbsp red wine vinegar
3 tbsp sour cream
salt and black pepper

Serves 4–6

Heat a small frying pan and gently toast the pine nuts. Empty them out of the pan as soon as they are lightly golden or they will continue to cook. Allow to cool while making the dressing.

Put the egg yolk and mustard into a bowl and whisk together. Slowly drizzle in the oils, whisking continuously so that they emulsify; if the oil is visible in the bowl stop drizzling and whisk until fully incorporated, then continue. Add the red wine vinegar and sour cream. Season with salt and pepper. If the dressing is very thick you can whisk in a little warm water.

Stir the pine nuts and raisins into the dressing and put aside for about an hour.

Peel the onion, cut in half and thinly slice. Sprinkle with a little salt and massage into the onion slices.

Wash the broccoli, drain well, and then chop it into roughly 2cm florets.

Put the broccoli and onion into a big bowl, pour the dressing over and mix well. Leave for an hour, if you can, before eating.

Red Cabbage, Celeriac, Apple and Hazelnut Salad

This is a great salad for the depths of winter. Deliciously crunchy, we make the dressing with an apple balsamic vinegar which perfectly complements the ingredients, but if you can't get your hands on it, just use a good wine vinegar.

150g hazelnuts
1 small red cabbage
1 red onion
1 dssp white wine vinegar
1 small celeriac
2 red apples
salt

Dressing
1 tsp Dijon mustard
50ml apple balsamic vinegar
75ml rapeseed or sunflower oil
75ml olive oil
salt

Serves 4–6

Preheat the oven to 180°C (350°F), Gas Mark 4. Roast the hazelnuts for about 10 minutes or until golden. Tip onto a tea towel and rub the skins off.

Finely slice the cabbage, put into a bowl and toss with a little salt. Set aside for at least 30 minutes, then pat dry.

Peel and finely slice the onion. Mix in a bowl with a pinch of salt and the wine vinegar and leave aside.

Peel and coarsely grate the celeriac and apples.

For the dressing, put the mustard into a small bowl, whisk in the apple balsamic followed by the oils and season with a little salt.

Put the vegetables into a bowl and toss together with the dressing. Serve immediately.

Raul's Catalan Artichokes with Aioli

1–2 small artichokes per person
lemon juice
olive oil
salt

Aioli
1 egg yolk
1 tsp Dijon mustard
2 cloves garlic, finely chopped
150ml olive oil
salt

Our house came with artichokes! When we arrived here thirty years ago there was a row of artichokes growing in one of our fields. We dug them up and moved them into our walled garden where they spring up like a seasonal hedge every year. We have divided them and shared them with friends over the years, and we have even planted some down on the road beside our entrance. We have also grown a few different varieties, some of which produce bigger and meatier artichokes. Baby and mature artichokes are both delicious to eat, but need to be prepared in different ways. One of the most popular ways to eat them in our household is as Raul's Catalan Artichokes. Raul is part of our extended family and he makes them the way his granny used to. They are prepared with our small variety of artichokes and it's an easy and unusual way to use them.

Wash the artichokes and snap off the outer layer of leaves until you reach the pale yellow layer. Trim the top centimetre or so if they are large, and cut off the stem. Cut the artichoke in half and with a spoon scoop out the hairy choke. Cut the flesh into quarters, then eighths. Drop into water with a squeeze of lemon juice to avoid discolouration while you prepare the rest of them. Pat dry before using.

To make the aioli, put the egg yolk, Dijon mustard and garlic into a bowl and slowly whisk in the olive oil, drip by drip, so that it emulsifies. Season with a little salt.

Heat a large skillet or frying pan and add about 1 centimetre of olive oil. Carefully slip in some artichoke pieces; don't overcrowd it, it's better to make them in smaller batches so they cook evenly. Keep the heat at medium and turn the artichokes until they are golden. Drain on kitchen paper and toss in a little salt.

Serve immediately with the aioli on the side for dipping.

Nectarine, Pink Peppercorn and Mint Tabbouleh

This delightful summery combination is an ideal salad for sunny days. Make when the nectarines are just ripe and the cucumbers are available locally. Mixed with mint, it's refreshing and bright. If you don't eat wheat, the bulgur can be swopped for quinoa.

300g bulgur wheat
300ml boiling water
1 red onion
1 cucumber
3 nectarines
big handful mint, chopped
1 lemon
handful pistachios
salt

Dressing
1 tsp pink peppercorns
1 tsp mustard
2–3 tbsp white balsamic vinegar
75ml olive oil
75ml rapeseed oil

Serves 4–6

For ease of measurement, place enough bulgur in a jug to reach the 300ml mark. Put into a bowl, add a little salt and pour the boiling water over. Give it a swirl and leave it while you chop the vegetables.

Peel and chop the red onion. Cut the cucumber into quarters lengthwise, remove the seeds, then cut each strip into half lengthwise again and dice into 1cm pieces.

Cut the nectarines in half around the stone, then give each half a firm wiggle in the opposite direction. With a bit of luck the nectarine will come apart, if not give it a little assistance with a small paring knife. Chop the nectarine into small dice.

Fluff the bulgur up with a fork or your hands.

Put the peppercorns into a mortar and give them a little bash with the pestle, just enough to rough them up. If you don't have a mortar and pestle put them in a bag and give them a gentle bash with a rolling pin.

For the dressing: put the mustard into a small bowl and whisk in the vinegar, oils and crushed peppercorns.

Check the bulgur – it should be cold by now. If it is, toss the vegetables with the bulgur and mint, then pour over the dressing and toss again. Check the seasoning and add a squeeze of lemon and a little more salt if necessary. Top with the pistachios.

Quinoa and Chickpea Salad

Quinoa is an ingredient with which people have become increasingly familiar. We use it a lot as it's versatile. When we first made quinoa salad we had a customer come back and say the salad was full of little worms which, with a massive stretch of the imagination, could describe this healthy little gem. It grows in South America and its soaring popularity is also making the price go up. Apparently it grows like a weed so hopefully the supply and demand will even out and we'll all be happy. Quinoa cooks very quickly so it's important not to overcook it, especially for a salad.

250g quinoa
375ml water
250g pumpkin or butternut squash
250g carrots
250g chickpeas, cooked (see p80)
1 red onion
½ cucumber
100g dried apricots
1 tbsp chopped coriander
olive oil
salt and black pepper

Dressing
1 tsp Dijon mustard
2 tbsp red wine vinegar
1 clove garlic
7 tbsp olive oil
1 heaped dssp runny honey
1 tsp ground cumin
1 tsp smoked paprika
salt

Serves 4–6

Preheat the oven to 180°C (350°F), Gas Mark 4.

Put the quinoa in a saucepan with the water and a little salt. Bring to the boil, cover with a lid, reduce the heat and simmer for 12–15 minutes. By then it will have absorbed the water, so tip into a bowl to cool.

Peel and chop the pumpkin into 2–3cm chunks. Peel the carrots, cut into half lengthwise, then half again so the carrots are in quarters and chop into chunks – not too small because they will shrink a little when they cook. Toss both the pumpkin and carrots in a little olive oil, season with salt and pepper and put into the oven to roast for about 20 minutes or until tender, then put aside to cool.

Put the quinoa, chickpeas, pumpkin and carrot into a large bowl. Peel and finely chop the red onion and add. Wash the cucumber and cut into quarters lengthwise. Remove the seeds and chop into 1cm dice. Add to the bowl. Season with salt and pepper.

Chop the dried apricots and add to the bowl with the coriander.

To make the dressing, put the Dijon mustard in a small bowl and whisk in the vinegar with a fork. Peel and finely chop the garlic, add to the bowl, then whisk in the olive oil and honey. Whisk in the cumin, smoked paprika and a little salt.

Pour the dressing over the salad and gently mix everything together.

Puy Lentil, Pea, Feta and Mint Salad

Puy lentils make great salads. Cooked properly, they hold together in their purple-blue casing and aren't at all mealy. Creamy hits of feta cheese with peas and mint mixed through keep this salad light and fresh.

200g Puy lentils
1 red onion
200g cherry tomatoes
100g feta
200g peas
handful fresh mint, chopped
salt

Dressing
1 tsp Dijon mustard
1 clove garlic, finely chopped
1 tbsp red wine vinegar
5–7 tbsp olive oil

Serves 4–6

Put the lentils into a saucepan and cover with water. Bring to the boil, cover with a lid and simmer for just under 20 minutes. Check and if they're not quite ready keep an eye on them because they will only take a couple more minutes. You want the lentils to be just done, tender but not mushy. Drain and rinse under a cold tap.

Peel and chop the onion. Halve or quarter the tomatoes. Chop the feta into cubes.

Blanch the peas for 1 minute in boiling, salted water, then drain and run under a cold tap. This applies to frozen peas too.

For the dressing, put the mustard and garlic into a small bowl and whisk in the vinegar, followed by the olive oil.

Put all the ingredients into a bowl and gently toss together with the mint and dressing. Season with salt and serve.

Summer Chickpea and Tuna Salad

This is one of those great salads that can be made by opening tins and jars. It's a very popular dish in Spain where they use an incredible amount of tinned beans and tuna in the kitchen. It is worth splashing out on a decent tin of tuna as you definitely get what you pay for. White tuna, also known as Bonito del Norte, is delicious (the Ortiz brand is particularly good) and quite different to standard tuna. This is used widely in Spain but isn't as well known here. It's worth seeking out. If you don't like tuna or are a vegetarian, substitute the tuna with 100g feta cheese.

2 large red peppers or 300g jar roasted peppers
1 small red onion
200g cherry tomatoes
1–2 tins chickpeas
1 x 112g tin tuna
handful fresh parsley
salt and pepper

Dressing
1–2 cloves garlic, peeled
2 tbsp sherry vinegar or red wine vinegar
4 tbsp extra virgin olive oil

Serves 4–6

If you are using fresh peppers you will need to roast them first. Preheat the oven to 200°C (400°F), Gas Mark 6 and place the peppers directly onto the shelf. Cook for 10 minutes, then turn and cook for a further 5-10 minutes. The peppers are ready when the skin is blistered. Take the peppers from the oven and pop them into a plastic bag. This will make them sweat and the skins will be easier to remove. When the peppers have cooled enough to handle, peel away the skins and remove the seeds. (If you are using a jar of roasted peppers, simply drain them.) Cut the peppers into long strips, then into approximately 5cm pieces.

Peel and chop the onion and halve or quarter the cherry tomatoes.

Drain the chickpeas and rinse. Drain the tin of tuna and flake with a fork.

Put all of the vegetables and the tuna into a serving bowl and season with a little salt and pepper.

For the dressing, finely chop the garlic and whisk together with the vinegar and olive oil.

Pour the dressing over the salad and gently toss together. Chop the parsley and scatter over the top. This salad is best served at room temperature.

New Potato and Smoked Mackerel Salad

Sunny weather usually means most people don't want to spend a lot of time cooking. This summer recipe uses new season potatoes, which are so welcome after the winter spuds. Some fresh herbs and locally smoked mackerel makes them into a feast. With a combination of sour cream and mayonnaise, the dressing is fresh and light. If you don't make your own mayonnaise, buy a good one. This dish is ideal for lunch, dinner or a barbeque and can be easily multiplied for a party.

500g new potatoes
4–5 spring onions
handful chopped dill or mint
175g smoked mackerel

Dressing
125ml mayonnaise
100ml sour cream
1 heaped dssp horseradish cream
salt and black pepper

Serves 2–3 as a main course
or 4–5 for a light lunch

Give the potatoes a scrub – there's no need to peel them – and put into a saucepan with cold water and a little salt. Bring to the boil, cover, and simmer until tender, probably 18–20 minutes, depending on the size of the potatoes.

For the dressing, mix the mayonnaise and sour cream together and stir in the horseradish. Season with salt and a few grinds of black pepper.

Chop the spring onions and the dill.

Peel the skin off the smoked mackerel and break the flesh into pieces.

Drain the cooked potatoes and allow to cool for a couple of minutes before cutting into bitesized chunks.

Put all the ingredients into a bowl and gently mix together. Check the seasoning.

Serve with dressed green leaves and tomatoes.

Som Tam

Whenever I go to Thailand I have a yen for Som Tam. This spicy, zesty salad is sold on the street, in the bus stations and at all the little restaurants. In fact it's pretty much everywhere. I find I read the menu from top to bottom with all the tempting noodles, seafood and curry dishes and still can't help but order it. Som Tam is like a Thai version of coleslaw, with crunchy julienned green papaya, a few shredded carrots and maybe some tomato and snapped up snake beans. It's healthier than coleslaw as the dressing is made with lime juice, chopped chillies, garlic and Thai fish sauce (nam pla). It's topped with a sprinkle of roasted and crushed peanuts. I have to admit this is part of the allure as I am something of a peanut fiend. I like to make this in Ireland but as green papayas are hard to come by I use green mangoes, which are plentiful and, I think, even tastier. I don't usually bother with the beans even though raw French beans make a reasonable substitute for the snake beans, and I usually skip the tomatoes they use too as Thai tomatoes are drier than the ones we get here. Dressed with the spicy sauce, this salad makes a fast and tasty lunch and will definitely add a spring to your step.

100g redskin peanuts (raw and unsalted)
1 tbsp dried shrimp (optional)
1 big green mango

Dressing
2–4 chillies
2–4 cloves garlic
juice 1–2 limes
2 tbsp Thai fish sauce
1 dssp sugar

Serves 4–6

Roast the peanuts on a tray in the oven at 180°C (350°F), Gas Mark 4, or dry fry in a pan until the skins rub off and the peanuts are light brown. It's important to roast the peanuts enough as it gives a better flavour. Tip the peanuts onto a clean tea towel and rub to remove the skins. Pick the peanuts out or take outside and blow the skins away. Crush coarsely in a mortar or bash in a plastic bag with a rolling pin.

Soak the shrimp, if using, in warm water for 10 minutes.

To make the dressing, chop the chillies and garlic together and mix with the lime juice, fish sauce and sugar.

Drain the shrimp, roughly chop, and then stir into the dressing.

Peel the mango, cut into thin slices, then into matchsticks (julienne).

Put the mango into a serving bowl, toss together with the dressing and sprinkle the peanuts on top.

Serve immediately.

Soups

Gazpacho 40

Spring Minestrone Soup 42

Spinach Soup 44

Leek, Sweet Potato and Spelt Soup 46

Thai Pumpkin Soup 48

Rooty Toot Soup 50

Gazpacho

This Spanish, chilled, tomato-based soup is pretty much a vegetable smoothie, apart from the fact that tomatoes are in fact a fruit. It should be made in the summer with vine ripened tomatoes. It needs to be served chilled so making it with tomatoes that have come out of the fridge will speed the whole process up. We don't usually keep our tomatoes in the fridge as in general they are best served at room temperature, but this soup is an exception. It's pretty much an instant lunch.

7–8 ripe tomatoes
2–3 small green peppers
½ small onion, finely chopped
½ regular cucumber
2–3 cloves garlic
1 slice white bread, crusts removed and soaked in cold water
3 tbsp good red wine vinegar
4–5 tbsp extra virgin olive oil
salt and black pepper
parsley, chopped

For the croutons:
2 slices decent white bread
1 clove garlic, cut in half
2 tbsp olive oil

Serves 4–6

Chop the vegetables, keeping a piece of green pepper aside for a garnish. Put them in a blender or liquidiser and purée until smooth.

Squeeze the excess water from the bread and add to the blender. Blend again.

Add the vinegar, oil, salt and pepper. Check the seasoning and chill.

To make some croutons, lightly toast 2 slices of bread, rub them with the garlic, then remove the crusts and brush with a little olive oil. Cut into small cubes and toss in a hot frying pan until golden.

Serve your gazpacho with the croutons, the reserved piece of pepper (finely chopped) and the parsley.

Spring Minestrone Soup

When I was a kid the only minestrone soup I knew came out of a tin; it was a tomato soup with well-cooked cubes of potato, carrot and peas. When I travelled to Italy I discovered that Italian minestrone and tinned minestrone are barely related. Tomatoes are in fact a small part of this soup and the recipe is infinitely variable. We use whatever seasonal vegetables we have to hand which might include a couple of ripe tomatoes but not always. I think there are two secrets to good minestrone. One is the addition of Parmesan rinds which give a great depth of flavour – meat eaters might disagree and prefer some fried pancetta or streaky bacon but either will enhance the soup. The other important factor is to gently sauté all the vegetables together before adding the stock. This helps each vegetable to taste sweeter and more intense. It's a great recipe for a hearty lunch or a lazy dinner and in our house it gets the Parmesan rinds out of the fridge where they would otherwise loll about indefinitely.

1 onion
25g butter
2 tbsp olive oil
2 stalks celery
1 bulb fennel
Parmesan rinds (optional)
1 leek
1 large carrot
1 large potato
2 large, ripe tomatoes, diced
sprig fresh rosemary
7–8 green cabbage leaves
1 litre vegetable or chicken stock
handful cooked cannellini beans
salt and pepper
Parmesan cheese

Serves 4–6

Peel and chop the onion. Heat a large saucepan, add the butter and olive oil, then the chopped onion. Cook on a high heat for a couple of minutes, then turn down the heat and cook gently with the lid off.

Cut the celery and fennel lengthwise and chop into 1–2cm dice. Add to the onions.

Add the Parmesan rinds, if using, and give everything a good stir.

Add the following vegetables to the pot as you chop them, stirring after each addition: the leek, cut lengthwise and rinsed under the tap to get rid of any soil, then chopped into 1cm pieces; the carrot, peeled and chopped into 1–2cm dice; the potato, peeled and cut into 1–2cm dice.

Season with a little salt and cook gently for 10–15 minutes.

Add the chopped tomatoes and when they have broken down to a pulp, stir in the chopped rosemary.

Shred the cabbage and add. Cook until the cabbage has wilted down – a few minutes.

Add the stock. Cook for 15 minutes.

Add the cannellini beans and cook for a further 10 minutes.

Season with salt and pepper.

If you have used Parmesan rinds fish them out before serving and discard.

If the soup is too thick, loosen it up with a little stock or water.

Serve with freshly grated Parmesan cheese.

Spinach Soup

We plant spinach both in tunnels and outside which gives us a constant supply for nine months of the year. If you are thinking of planting some vegetables, perpetual spinach should be high up your list as it's a trouble-free, high-producer of fantastic green leaves. This soup is fast to make, inexpensive and nutritious. If you have a problem with wheat, use a potato instead of the flour to thicken the soup: one large potato, sautéed with the onion, then cooked in the stock before adding the spinach will do the trick.

1 onion
50g butter
2 tbsp white flour
600ml chicken or vegetable stock
400ml milk
500g spinach
freshly grated nutmeg
salt and black pepper
cream to serve (optional)

Serves 4–6

Peel and chop the onion. Melt the butter in a saucepan and gently sauté the onions until they soften.

Add the flour and stir for a couple of minutes, then whisk in the stock and milk. Keep stirring until the soup comes to the boil.

Wash and roughly chop the spinach, then add it to the boiling stock.

Add a couple of grates of nutmeg and season with salt and black pepper. As soon as the spinach wilts and the soup returns to the boil, take it off the heat and liquidise.

Check the seasoning and serve with a swirl of cream.

Leek, Sweet Potato and Spelt Soup

Pearled spelt is an ancient variety of wheat, similar to the Italian grain farro, and is great in soups, stews and risottos. When I was a child my mum used to make a soup with that Sunday's leftover roast chicken carcass, vegetables and pearl barley. It was a regular Monday dinner, and this soup is a vegetarian version of that childhood favourite. Of course, if you have a roast chicken carcass handy, throw it in.

1 large onion
2 tbsp olive oil
2 sticks celery
1 carrot
1 sweet potato
2 leeks
75g pearled spelt
1 litre vegetable or chicken stock
salt and black pepper
handful parsley

Serves 4–6

Peel and finely chop the onion. Heat a large saucepan and add the olive oil and onion.

Add the following vegetables to the saucepan as you chop them.

Wash and trim the celery, cut into half lengthwise, then chop into 1cm dice.

Peel the carrot, cut into quarters lengthwise, and then chop into 1cm dice.

Peel the sweet potato and cut into 2cm dice.

Trim the leeks and wash well under a running tap. Chop into 1cm lengths and add to the pot. Give everything a stir, add a little salt and leave to cook gently until the vegetables begin to soften.

Stir in the pearled spelt and the stock or water and chicken carcass. Bring to the boil, then turn the heat down and simmer for about twenty minutes, until the vegetables and spelt are tender. Season with salt and pepper.

Chop the parsley, including stalks, and stir into the soup.

Serve as it is unless you used a chicken carcass, in which case fish it out and throw away before serving.

Thai Pumpkin Soup

Pumpkins are one of our main crops and they grow in their own armoured casings. Our favourites are the varieties Queensland Blue and Crown Prince both of which produce a dense, dark, yellow flesh and have very good flavour. They are harvested in late September and store well until we eat our way through them, which could be as late as February or March if they're in a cool, dry place. It's highly unlikely we would ever have too many left as the pumpkin is a very versatile and nutritious vegetable; it can be used to make soups, cakes, chutneys and curries, or simply roasted. This recipe uses Thai flavours and coconut milk to make a smooth and fragrant soup.

1 onion
2 stalks celery
1 carrot
500g pumpkin
2–3 cloves garlic
3cm piece fresh ginger
rapeseed or sunflower oil
1 level dssp Thai curry paste, red or green

1 litre vegetable stock
75g red lentils
2–3 lime leaves
100g creamed coconut
1 tbsp Thai fish sauce
handful fresh coriander

Serves 4–6

Chop the onion, celery and carrot into 1cm dice, and the pumpkin into 2cm dice. Finely chop the garlic and ginger.

Heat a tablespoon of oil in a saucepan and add the onion and celery. Cook for a couple of minutes, then add the garlic and ginger followed by the Thai curry paste, carrot and pumpkin. Cook everything together for about 5 minutes or until the vegetables begin to soften.

Add the stock, lentils, lime leaves, coconut and fish sauce. Bring to the boil then simmer for 15-20 minutes, until the vegetables are tender.

Buzz until smooth, then stir in the chopped coriander and check the seasoning. Before serving, add more fish sauce or salt if necessary.

Rooty Toot Soup

This is a bottom of the vegetable basket type soup – just chuck in whatever you have. It's a flexible recipe and is very easy to make. It's just a matter of sweating the vegetables and adding stock. We add a little garam masala, just enough to make you wonder what the extra flavour is, and a handful of red lentils. It also freezes well: just pour into ziplock freezer bags and stack flat in your freezer.

1 onion
2 tbsp vegetable or olive oil
2 stalks celery
3 carrots
1 small parsnip
½ celeriac
1 small sweet potato (optional)

1 litre stock – vegetable or chicken
1 tsp garam masala
100g red lentils
salt and pepper
chopped parsley or coriander to serve

Serves 4–6

Peel and chop the onion. Heat a saucepan and add the oil and onions. Give them a stir, then chop the celery and add.

Keep the vegetables cooking without browning, turn the heat down if necessary, while you peel and chop all the root vegetables into even-sized pieces and add to the pan.

Season with a little salt and cook gently for about 5 minutes, then add the stock, garam masala and lentils.

Bring the soup to the boil, then reduce the heat and simmer for 15–20 minutes, until the vegetables are tender.

Buzz the soup to a smooth purée and season with salt and pepper. If the soup is too thick, thin with a little water.

Serve with a little chopped parsley or coriander and a swirl of cream if you fancy.

Fishy Dishes

Fish en Papillote 54

Thai Sweet and Sour Mackerel 56

Fish in Pakora Batter with Spicy Wedges 58

Grilled Cod with Roasted Cherry Tomatoes and Basil 60

Grilled Prawns with Whiskey Mayonnaise 62

Moroccan Fish Tagine 64

Red Curry over Fish 66

Seafood Chowder 68

Suquet de Peix 70

Fish Stock 72

Fish en Papillote (Fish in Parchment)

Fish cooked in a parcel, in this instance on a bed of vegetables, is tasty, healthy and easy to prepare. The vegetables are cut into matchsticks, gently cooked in a little butter and dressed with ginger. The fish sits on top of the vegetables, enclosed in a paper parcel and cooks in its own juices. Ask your fishmonger to give you plump steaks from the top end of the fish rather than skinny pieces from the tail.

600g chunky fish (hake, cod, salmon or ling)
1 carrot
1 onion
1 leek
1 small courgette
25g butter
25g piece fresh ginger
salt and pepper
lemon juice

Serves 4

Cut the fish into four portion sizes and remove any stray bones.

Peel the carrot and onion and wash the leek and courgette. Cut the onion in half and slice thinly. Cut the carrot, leek and courgettes into thin slices lengthways and then into matchsticks.

Melt the butter in a frying pan and add the vegetables. Season with a little salt and pepper and toss around to coat well. Once you can hear the vegetables cooking, turn the heat to medium, then cook gently for a few minutes, until they have softened.

Grate the ginger without peeling on the coarse side of the grater. Gather the ginger into your hands and squeeze the juice over the vegetables. Discard the ginger. Check the seasoning then put the vegetables aside to cool.

Using a large dinner plate or something similar cut a circle of parchment paper for the fish. Place a small mound of vegetables just off-centre and the fish on top. Season the fish with salt and pepper and a little squeeze of lemon juice. Carefully close the parcel by bringing the sides together and double folding to make a sealed parcel, twisting the edges together as you go. Put on a baking tray and either leave in the fridge until needed or place into a preheated oven, 180°C (350°F), Gas Mark 4. Cook for 12–15 minutes.

Put the parcel on a plate and serve with twists of lemon.

Thai Sweet and Sour Mackerel

We found this recipe on our first visit to Thailand when we were staying on a beach near Krabi. The family that ran the 'bungalows' where we were based made delicious food. Every day there was fresh fish on the menu and we often ate our fish 'sweet and sour', with a tart but sweet sauce that has a lively kick. We quizzed Kong, the chef, about the recipe and when he explained, it was so simple it was difficult to believe that was all there was to it: just five ingredients and some fish. This was also the place where I learned how to use tamarind in cooking. Kong explained that he used tamarind whenever something was in need of a little sour acidity because limes were expensive. Tamarind is easy to find these days and can be bought as a lump of dried pods or as a concentrate. For this recipe I prefer the concentrate as it's easier to use. One teaspoon of concentrate mixed with boiling water will make about 50ml of tamarind juice. If you are using dried pods, crumble a few into a small bowl and cover with boiling water. Squish the pods about with a wooden spoon then leave for ten minutes. To use, strain and give the pods a good mash with a wooden spoon for maximum extraction. We usually have this sauce with mackerel but it works equally well with salmon.

4 mackerel, filleted
7 cloves garlic
4 red chillies
50ml tamarind juice
50ml Thai fish sauce

50g sugar
oil to fry
handful fresh coriander, chopped

Serves 4

Place the mackerel fillets on a chopping board and carefully cut out the central strip of bones by cutting along each side of the strip, without cutting through the skin at the back. Pick the fillet up and you should be able to pinch the top of the strip and pull it down and away from the skin in one go, like pulling a plaster off quickly. Check the mackerel fillets for any other stray bones and put aside.

Peel and chop the garlic and chop together with the chillies.

Mix the tamarind, fish sauce and sugar together.

Heat a pan, add a little oil to coat the bottom of the pan and fry the mackerel, skin side down, for a few minutes, then turn and cook the other side. Transfer to a warmed serving dish.

Put a little more oil in the pan and fry the garlic and chilli together for a couple of minutes. Don't let the garlic burn. Add the tamarind/fish sauce/sugar mix and allow to bubble up and reduce.

Add the coriander, give the pan a swirl and pour over the fish. Serve with rice to mop up the sauce.

Fish in Pakora Batter with Spicy Wedges

This is the same batter mix that I use to make vegetable pakoras. We had a bit of fish left over one weekend and I cut it into 2cm pieces, dunked it in the batter and deep-fried it. It worked wonderfully. The fish was delicious and perfectly cooked inside the crisp batter. We ate it with a little raita (yoghurt and cucumber) on the side but I reckon it would also be good with homemade mayo with a little garam masala stirred in. Pakoras are made with gram flour (a gluten-free flour made of ground chickpeas) which gives an interesting batter but if you prefer you could substitute plain white flour.

4 x 150g fresh white fish
4 heaped tbsp gram flour
(or plain white flour)
½ tsp salt
1 tsp baking powder
1–2 red chillies, finely chopped
1 dssp crushed coriander seeds
or 1 tsp garam masala
small bottle or can chilled beer
500ml vegetable/sunflower/rapeseed oil
for frying

Spicy Potato Wedges
16–20 small potatoes
2 tbsp olive oil
1 tsp paprika
½ tsp chilli flakes
salt

Serves 4

Preheat the oven to 180°C (350°F), Gas Mark 4.

First, make the spicy potato wedges. Wash the potatoes and cut into quarters – no need to peel. Put into a bowl and toss with the olive oil. Sprinkle with the paprika and chilli flakes and toss again. Season with a little salt. Tip onto an oven tray, keeping them in a single layer. Bake for 15 minutes, then give the tray a shake and bake for a further 15 minutes or until lightly crisp.

Cut the fish into 2cm pieces.

Sieve the gram flour into a bowl together with the salt and baking powder, chilli and spice. Slowly whisk in some beer until you get a thick pouring batter. The batter should fall off the spoon in a thick stream. If it falls off in lumps, thin it with a little more beer. If it's too runny, just sieve in a little more flour.

Carefully heat the oil in a wok, deep-fat-fryer or saucepan. Test it's hot enough by dropping a cube of bread, piece of onion or other vegetable into the oil. When it comes back quickly to the surface the oil is ready.

Season the fish with a little salt and drop into the batter, mixing around to cover the fish completely. Carefully lower each piece into the hot oil, cooking no more than 5 or 6 pieces at a time, otherwise the oil temperature will fluctuate too much and the batter will cook unevenly. Turn the pieces after a minute or two and when nicely browned remove and drain on kitchen paper.

Eat immediately with a serving of spicy wedges.

Grilled Cod with Roasted Cherry Tomatoes and Basil

This recipe is great in summer and very quick to make. Just be sure the tomatoes are ripe and the oven is hot before you begin cooking.

300g cherry tomatoes
4 pieces of cod, about 150g each
1 lemon
handful basil
olive oil
salt and black pepper

Serves 4

Preheat the oven to 200°C (400°F), Gas Mark 6.

Toss the tomatoes in a little olive oil and season with salt and pepper. Put them in a roasting pan or ovenproof dish and roast for 10 minutes.

Heat a heavy ovenproof frying pan or grill pan until hot. Check the fish for any stray bones, leave the skin on and drizzle with a little olive oil. Season with salt and pepper. Put the fish fillets skin side down on the hot pan. Leave for 4–5 minutes, depending on the thickness of each piece of fish. You should be able to see the fish turning opaque as it cooks. Turn the fish over and pop the pan into the oven (at the same temperature as the tomatoes) and cook for a further 3 minutes. Turn the heat off and leave the fish to relax while you finish the sauce.

Cut the lemon in half. Reserve one part and cut the other into wedges.

At this stage the tomatoes should be ready. The skins will have burst and the juices beginning to run. Take out of the oven and stir in the basil and the juice of the half-lemon.

Put a portion of fish onto each plate and spoon the tomato-basil sauce on top. Serve with a lemon wedge.

Grilled Prawns with Whiskey Mayonnaise

This dish was really popular when we had our restaurant and was one of which we could never have too much. We use Dublin Bay Prawns and it is imperative that the prawns are spanking fresh – alive is best. If you are squeamish you will have to get someone else to take the heads off for you. If you can't find live prawns, watch that the prawns are bright eyed, a healthy pink and not smelling of anything but the sea. And finally, in this case, the bigger the better. If you can find good, fatty prawns you will only need three or four per person. Prepare yourself for a treat!

3–5 big Dublin Bay prawns
1 large clove garlic
coarsely ground black pepper
olive oil
salad leaves, tomatoes and lemon wedges to serve

Whiskey Mayonnaise
2 egg yolks
1 tsp Dijon mustard
200ml sunflower or rapeseed oil
50ml olive oil
1 tsp tomato purée
1–2 cloves garlic, finely chopped
salt and black pepper
1 tbsp/capful whiskey

Serves 1

First, you need to butterfly the prawns. Crack the head off each prawn and stash them in the fridge or freezer for later use in a stock. Put the prawn belly side up on the chopping board, stretch it out, and with a sharp knife cut through the light part of the translucent shell lengthwise, through the flesh, but don't cut through the shell at the other side. Turn the prawn over and with the heel of your hand crack the shell so that the prawn splays out. Gently remove any dark vein of intestine that you can find. Do this to all the prawns, then put them into a shallow dish *shell side down*.

Peel and finely chop the garlic and scatter over the prawns with some black pepper, then drizzle with olive oil. Mix with your fingers to get all the flavours together, then cover and put in the fridge for about 1 hour.

Now to make the whiskey mayonnaise: the following method is the traditional way to make it with a whisk, but a blender works well when the ingredients are added in the same order and the oils dripped in slowly.

Put the egg yolks and mustard into a small bowl and whisk together. Whisk in a little sunflower oil, allowing it to emulsify with the egg yolks before adding a little more. Whisk in the olive oil, tomato purée, garlic, salt and pepper, and whiskey. Don't be tempted to exceed the amount of whiskey as too much will overpower the flavour.

To grill the prawns, preheat the grill pan (a cast-iron grill pan is best but otherwise use your heaviest frying pan). Make sure the grill pan is hot. Put the prawns belly side down on the pan and push them down to splay out. Cook for 1–2 minutes, then turn over and roast on the shell side for 4–5 minutes.

Prepare a plate for each person with salad leaves, wedges of tomato and lemon. Put the whiskey mayo into small dipping bowls, or a larger bowl to share. Put the prawns, shell side down, tails to the outside of the plate between the tomatoes and lemons, and serve.

Moroccan Fish Tagine

We discovered this little one-pot gem when we were in Morocco. I was lucky enough to join the ladies cooking in the kitchen while Con was banished to the parlour to drink mint tea. The kitchen was very basic and the tagine was cooked on a charcoal fire. The women quickly prepared the vegetables, assembled the dish in layers, covered it and left it to cook slowly. A tagine is a good-looking two-piece earthenware cooking vessel with a conical lid that captures all the steam and juices from the simmering dish. This is, of course, just what a casserole does, so if you don't have a tagine, use a casserole with a lid or a roasting tin covered with some aluminium foil. Although the list of ingredients looks long, there are only two simple steps involved in making this dish. First make the charmoula, the marinade, with plenty of fresh herbs, then prepare the vegetables. Use any firm white fish; thick fillets are ideal.

600g white fish (e.g. cod, hake) divided into 4 portions
good pinch saffron
100ml hot water
2–3 large potatoes
3 tbsp olive oil
1 green pepper
4 ripe tomatoes
or 1 x 400g tin whole tomatoes
4 tbsp cold water

Charmoula Marinade
4 cloves garlic, finely chopped
1 small onion, finely chopped
3 tbsp chopped parsley
3 tbsp chopped coriander
4 tbsp olive oil
½ tsp salt
1 tsp paprika
1 tsp cumin
¼ tsp cinnamon
juice ½ lemon

Serves 4

Preheat the oven to 180°C (350°F), Gas Mark 4.

To make the marinade, simply put all the ingredients into a bowl and mix together.

Put the fish pieces into the marinade, give them a turn so they are well coated and set aside.

Drop the saffron into the hot water and leave it to infuse.

Peel and finely slice the potatoes. Pour the olive oil into the tagine or casserole and add the potatoes in a layer. Season with a little salt. De-seed and thinly slice the green pepper and put over the potatoes. Chop the tomatoes and scatter on top.

Take the fish out of the marinade and place on a new plate in the fridge.

Mix the saffron-infusing water with the marinade and pour half over the vegetables in the tagine. Cover the pot and cook in the oven for 1 hour.

Remove from the oven, uncover and arrange the fish on top.

Mix the remaining marinade with about 4 tbsp water and drizzle it over everything. Put the cover back on and cook for a further 20–25 minutes.

Take out of the oven and carefully remove the lid to avoid being scorched by the steam. Give the fish a gentle poke to check it is cooked.

Serve with crusty bread.

Red Curry over Fish

The lady who does the cooking where we stayed in Thailand makes this dish. It's not a big bowl of soupy red curry, rather a sauce laced with coconut, spices and herbs, poured on top of fried fish and finished with stir-fried veg and rice – totally delicious. At home we make this with cod, hake or monkfish; the original version was barracuda but that's not available in our locality. Making fresh curry paste might seem like a lot of trouble but the most difficult part is usually gathering the ingredients. Unless you live close by an Asian market it can be a problem. Whenever I go to the city I do a bulk buy and then keep a stash in my freezer. Lemongrass, galangal and lime leaves all freeze well, even chillies do, if you don't mind them being a little soggy when they defrost. Fresh lime leaves aren't always available but dried ones will do if you're stuck. This is all well worth the effort as fresh curry paste is zippy and fragrant.

2 tbsp red curry paste
200ml coconut milk
1 tsp palm sugar or light muscovado
1–2 tbsp Thai fish sauce
150–200g fish per person (cod, hake or monkfish)
juice ½ lime
handful chopped fresh coriander
sunflower or rapeseed oil

Thai Red Curry Paste
10 big dried red chillies, seeds removed
1 tbsp coriander seeds
3 cardamom pods
½ tsp black peppercorns
½ tsp salt
2cm galangal (substitute ginger if necessary)
5 kaffir lime leaves, finely chopped
2 stems lemongrass, finely chopped
3 shallots, peeled and chopped
6–7 cloves garlic, peeled and chopped
1 tsp shrimp paste
6–10 small red chillies, chopped

Serves 3–4

First you need to make the curry paste. Soak the dried chillies in a little water for at least ten minutes.

Roast the coriander seeds and cardamom pods in a dry frying pan until light brown and fragrant. Allow them to cool then put them, and the peppercorns, into a coffee grinder (or mortar and pestle) and grind until fine. Pick out and discard the rough part of the cardamom pods as they become loose.

Drain the dried chillies, roughly chop and put into a blender or mortar with the remaining ingredients, except for the ground spices, and mix until you have a smooth paste. If using a blender you'll probably need to add a little water to achieve this. Finally add in the ground spices and mix until smooth.

This recipe makes enough for about three batches of this dish; it can be stored in the fridge for a week in a sealed container or frozen in three portions. It can be used to make any type of Thai red curry.

Put a little oil in a small pan and fry 2 tbsp curry paste for a minute or two. Don't let it burn.

Stir in the coconut milk and palm sugar and season with the fish sauce. Set aside.

If you are using cod or hake or something similar it's probably easier to leave the skin on but monkfish needs to have the outer membrane taken off. Season the fish with salt and drizzle a little oil over each portion.

Heat a heavy pan or a ridged grill pan. When the pan is very hot put the fish in, skin side down, and leave for 4–5 minutes, depending on the thickness of the fish. You will see the fish going opaque as it cooks. When it looks half cooked, carefully turn each piece over and cook for a few minutes on the other side.

Re-heat the sauce, season with the lime juice and stir in some chopped coriander.

Put the fish on warm plates and pour over a little sauce. Garnish with chopped coriander and serve with basmati or jasmine rice. Stir-fried mangetout, green beans and courgette batons are delicious on top.

Seafood Chowder

Seafood chowder is a warm and satisfying dish which leaves very little washing up. The fish stock is the only component that will cause any complications. It is easy to make but it does need fish bones which means a visit to the fishmonger or the market.
If this isn't possible just use chicken or vegetable stock. If you are using mussels soak them in a bowl of clean water for an hour before using, if you have time, and if you don't like mussels add more fish. This recipe makes a hearty dinner for two or a bowl of soup for four.

1 onion
1–2 potatoes
1–2 carrots
30g butter
30g flour
500ml fish stock (see page 72)
500ml milk
1 bay leaf
pinch cayenne
pinch nutmeg
salt and pepper
500g fresh mussels (optional)
splash wine or water
300–500g fresh fish
cream to serve

Serves 2–4

Peel and chop the onion. Peel and dice the potato and carrot into 1cm dice.

Melt the butter in a small saucepan and when it begins to bubble add the chopped onion. Cook the onion gently until it softens, then add the flour to make a roux. Stir for a couple of minutes making sure that the flour cooks well, but doesn't burn.

Whisk in the fish stock and milk and continue to stir until it comes to the boil. Add the potatoes, carrot, bay leaf, cayenne and nutmeg. Season with salt and pepper. Cook gently for a further 10–15 minutes until the potato and carrot are tender.

This is the base for your chowder. If you are ready to eat, continue, otherwise chill the base and re-heat when you are ready.

If you are using mussels, make sure they are well scrubbed and all tightly closed. If they are stuck open or damaged, discard them as they are probably dead. Put them into a saucepan together with a splash of white wine or water and place onto a high heat. Cover with a tight lid and shake until all the mussels open. This will only take a few minutes. Remove the mussels from their shells and strain off the cooking broth. The broth can be added to the chowder base but be cautious as it may be salty.

Chop the fresh fish into even-sized chunks. Add the fish pieces to the chowder, allow to bubble away for a couple of minutes, then stir in the mussels.

Cook for one minute more, then serve immediately with a little swirl of cream.

For the picada, remove the crusts from the bread and cut into 1cm cubes. Heat a little olive oil in a pan and fry the bread until golden. Put the almonds into a bowl and cover with boiling water for a few minutes, then refresh with cold water. The skins of the almonds should now slip off. Put the fried bread, almonds and garlic into a food processor and buzz to a fine crumb (or mash together with a mortar and pestle). Slowly pour in enough olive oil to make a loose paste. Season with a little salt. Chop the parsley and stir in.

Peel and chop the onions. De-seed and chop the peppers into about 2cm dice. Peel and finely chop the garlic. Peel and cut the potatoes into 3cm chunks.

In a large pot cook the onions and peppers in a little olive oil until soft. Add the chopped garlic and cook on medium heat for a couple of minutes. Add the potatoes and cook for 5 minutes. Chop or grate the tomatoes on the coarse side of a grater, and add to the pot. Cook gently until the tomatoes break down.

Add the brandy or wine, followed by the fish stock. Continue cooking until the potatoes are tender. Season with salt and pepper. Leave to one side.

Clean the mussels and remove the beards. Discard any that are damaged or open. Skin the monkfish and cut into medallions about 1cm thick or cut the hake into four steaks – ideally your fishmonger will do this for you.

Put the stew back on the heat and stir in 1 tablespoon of the picada. Add the monkfish and then scatter over the mussels. (If you are using hake, cook for a couple of minutes before adding the mussels.) When the stew returns to the boil, turn it down. As soon as the mussels open, remove from the heat. Adjust the seasoning and serve with the remaining picada in a bowl on the side.

Suquet de Peix (Catalan Fish Stew)

We first encountered this dish in Cadaqués on the Costa Brava – the town that is otherwise famous as where Salvador Dalí lived for most of his adult life. It is traditionally made with clams and fish but I use mussels as clams are hard to come by where we live. Sometimes I use monkfish and other times I use small steaks of hake cut on the bone. It depends on what is winking at me on the fishmonger's slab and how affluent I am feeling that day but you can use whatever fish and shellfish you like. Essentially it's a one pot dinner but a great dish for entertaining as the basic stew can be made and then left aside until the guests arrive when you can reheat the stew and pop the fish in. It is served with a parsley and almond picada – a sauce similar to a pesto.

2 onions
2 red peppers
4 cloves garlic
6 waxy potatoes
4 large tomatoes or 1 x 400g tin tomatoes
⅓ glass brandy or 1 glass white wine
750ml fish stock (see page 72)
500g mussels or clams
600g monkfish or 800g hake on the bone
olive oil
salt and pepper

Picada
1 slice white bread
30 almonds
2 cloves garlic, finely chopped
olive oil
salt
small bunch parsley

Serves 4–6

Fish Stock

Making fish stock is easy, it's finding the fish bones and heads that can be difficult. Independent fish shops and markets are probably the best places to look. Big stores buy in fish that's filleted at sea and they don't usually have bins of bones to hand. In Spain, where they eat a lot of fish, bones and heads are a valued commodity and buying fish will often include getting the bones and head for the caldo which is their stock. When I make fish stock I make a big batch and freeze it in several portions for future use. To make a good stock you need to use bones from white, not oily fish. The best bones are from turbot or brill, but plaice, sole, John Dory, cod and hake will all do; fish heads are a bonus.

1 kg fish bones
1 celery stick
1 carrot
1 onion
1 leek, white part only (optional)
4–5 stalks parsley

Serves 4–6

Wash the fish bones and remove any trace of guts and blood. Put into a large saucepan.

Chop the celery, carrot, onion and leek. Add to the pot with the parsley and cover with water. The water should just cover the vegetables and bones, it doesn't need to be swimming.

Put the pot on a high heat and when it comes to the boil turn down to a simmer for 15–20 minutes. Turn the heat off and leave to rest, if you have time, before straining. Use immediately or freeze for future use in sauces and for the seafood chowder on page 68.

Chorizo Infiltration

Chorizo and Bean Soup with Kale 76

Potato and Chorizo Tart 78

Chickpeas and Chorizo 80

Chorizo and Cabbage Paella 82

Chorizo and Bean Soup with Kale

Chorizo is an amazingly versatile and tasty Spanish sausage. We love using it as a flavour enhancer. A couple of chorizo in any soup or stew will add another dimension without giving you a pile of meat to chomp through. It's made all over Spain, in Mexico, Portugal and, most surprisingly (for me when I found it) in Goa; although if you know your history it's hardly surprising as Goa was once upon a time a Portuguese colony. This recipe was inspired by the abundant kale in our garden and is a variation on a Spanish classic: beans and chorizo. It's a very versatile recipe, as the cannellini beans can be exchanged for butterbeans or chickpeas, and if you don't have kale, you can try half a savoy cabbage. For a vegetarian version leave out the chorizo and substitute a teaspoon of smoked paprika. There are a couple of advantages in cooking your own beans, one being that they are far more economical and the other that the cooking liquid helps to make a tasty stock.

450g cannellini beans or 2 x 400g tins
1 litre vegetable stock
1 medium onion
3 tbsp olive oil
2 stalks celery
2 carrots
2 cloves garlic
200g fresh chorizo
12–14 kale leaves or half a small savoy cabbage
1 tin tomatoes
salt and pepper

Serves 4–6

If you are using dried beans soak them overnight in plenty of cold water. For tinned beans, simply drain and rinse before use. Put them in a saucepan the next day, making sure the water level comes up at least 2cm above the beans and bring to the boil. Turn down to a simmer and put the lid on. Do not add salt. Cannellini beans and butterbeans will take between 45–90 minutes to cook and the chickpeas anything from 1–3 hours. Top up with water if necessary. The beans need to end up tender but still keep their shape.

When they are cooked, drain them and reserve the cooking liquid to make the vegetable stock; you might have to top up with water to make the required amount of stock for this recipe.

Peel and chop the onion into 1cm dice. Put a saucepan on the heat and pour in the olive oil. Add the onions, turn the heat to medium and let the onions sizzle.

Wash the celery, cut into three lengthways, and then chop into 1cm dice and add to the saucepan.

Peel the carrots and cut into quarters lengthwise and chop these into a dice. Add these to the onions, season with a little salt, and give a stir.

Peel and chop the garlic, and when the vegetables have sweated for about 5 minutes, add to the pan.

Cut the chorizo into half lengthwise, then chop into 2cm pieces. Stir into the vegetables and cook until the oils run from the chorizo. The oil will give a lovely red hue to everything.

Shred the kale into ribbons and stir in. Cook until it begins to wilt.

Add the tomatoes, roughly chopped, followed by the stock and cannellini beans.

Season with salt and pepper. If you are using tinned beans you will need less salt. Bring to the boil and simmer for about 20 minutes.

Serve with crusty bread or spuds for a more substantial meal.

Potato and Chorizo Tart

Chorizo sautéed with red onion and peppers slowly releases tasty red juices, and when diced potatoes are added they gobble up the flavours. This makes a delicious tart filling. Sometimes we use Puy lentils instead of potatoes - this works very well too - but potato is the more popular version in our shop.
If you want to try Puy lentils instead of potatoes substitute 150g cooked lentils.

2–3 red onions
1 small red pepper
200–250g fresh chorizo sausages
3 medium potatoes, cooked
4 eggs
200ml cream
200ml milk
olive oil
salt and black pepper
1 x 24–28cm pre-baked pastry case (see page 132)

Serves 4–6

Preheat the oven to 180°C (350°F), Gas Mark 4.

Peel and thinly slice the red onions. Wash the red pepper, cut in half, remove the seeds and slice into thin strips.

Heat a frying pan, add enough olive oil to barely cover the bottom, and add the onions and pepper. Cook on a high heat until they are sizzling, then lower the heat to medium. Season with a little salt. Cook for 15 minutes, giving the odd stir to prevent them from sticking to the pan and burning.

Slice the chorizo sausages into small pieces and add to the pan. Increase the heat until everything is sizzling once more. Cook until the oil runs from the chorizo – about 10 minutes. Turn the heat down if it begins to stick.

Dice the cooked potatoes and stir into the vegetable/chorizo mix.

Crack the eggs into a bowl, then whisk in the cream and milk. Season with 1 level tsp salt and ¼ tsp pepper.

Spread the cooled vegetables/chorizo onto the pastry base and pour over the egg mixture. Fill to just under the top of the pastry to avoid the possibility of spillage which would make the pastry soggy.

Bake for 20–25 minutes, until the filling is golden and set.

Chickpeas and Chorizo

This is pretty much a no-fail recipe and it's found in lots of traditional bars in Spain where I first experienced the chorizo revelation. Being a vegetarian on holiday is not always the easiest. Some cultures just don't get it, and it's difficult to find a good variety of food. I found myself looking longingly at the chickpea stews and, being a very casual vegetarian, decided to eat my way around the chorizo. It was very tasty and I have been eating it occasionally ever since. This makes a quick and nutritious family dinner.

Peel and chop the onion and gently sauté in the olive oil.

Wash the celery, slice lengthwise, then chop and add to the pan.

Chop the peppers and add, all the time cooking gently so the vegetables soften.

Add the garlic, peeled and chopped.

Cut the chorizo into 1cm slices and add to the pan. Cook gently until the chorizo begins to release its oil.

Add the cooked chickpeas and tomatoes and bring to the boil. If the mixture looks thick or likely to stick to the pan, you may need to add a little water or reserved cooking liquid from the chickpeas, if you cooked them yourself. Season with salt and pepper and simmer for 15–20 minutes.

Sprinkle with parsley before serving.

*To cook chickpeas from dried, cover well with cold water and leave overnight. Drain and re-cover with water to about twice the depth of the chickpeas. Bring to the boil and simmer gently for 40–90 minutes, until tender. The cooking time will depend on how old the chickpeas are. Test and continue to cook if necessary. Do not add salt until the chickpeas have finished cooking as this will seriously slow the cooking process. They can be cooled and frozen for later use.

1 large onion
2 tbsp olive oil
2–3 stalks celery
1 red pepper
1 green pepper
3–4 cloves garlic
200–250g chorizo sausages
400g cooked chickpeas *
500g tomatoes or 400g tin chopped tomatoes
salt and pepper
chopped parsley to serve

Serves 4–6

Chorizo and Cabbage Paella

The origin of paella wasn't a fancy dish full of shellfish and chicken, it was a dish cooked at the end of the week when the cupboards were a bit bare, to use up odds and ends. Obviously if you lived by the sea you might have fishy bits, but inland the paellas would use chorizo, rabbit, pork, chicken and whatever vegetables were handy. This recipe is our own aberration, cooked up one night for a crowd when there was very little else in the cupboard.

2 medium onions
2–3 celery stalks
2 peppers, any colour
1 leek, white part only
4 cloves garlic
200–250g fresh chorizo
300g calasparra rice (or arborio)
1 x 400g tin chopped tomatoes
1 tsp smoked paprika
125ml white wine
800ml vegetable or chicken stock
½ green cabbage
1 dssp soy sauce
olive oil
salt and black pepper

Serves 4–6

Peel and chop the onions. Heat a large wide-based frying pan and add enough olive oil to cover the bottom (about 100ml). Add the onions and stir. Season with a little salt.

Cut the celery into 2 or 3 strips lengthwise, then dice into 1cm pieces. Add to the onion in the pan and continue cooking. It's important to maintain the heat so the vegetables are sizzling away but without browning. Stir frequently.

De-seed the peppers and chop into 3cm dice, add to the pan, season with a little salt and stir.

Chop the leek and add to the rest of the vegetables. Give a good grind of black pepper and check the seasoning.

Peel and chop the garlic and add to the pan.

Cut the chorizo in half lengthways. Chop the chorizo into equal-sized chunks of about 1–2cm and add to the pan. Cook until the oils from the chorizo are released.

Stir in the rice and cook for a couple of minutes, then add the tomatoes, smoked paprika and white wine. Bring the temperature up so that the alcohol burns off, then stir in the stock. Taste and adjust seasoning. Once it comes to the boil, turn down to maintain a slow bubbling. Now stand back and do not stir. Cook gently for about 16 minutes, then turn the heat off. Cover with a piece of aluminium foil and leave to relax.

Shred the cabbage and stir-fry in a little oil for a few minutes then add the soy sauce and about a dessertspoon of water. Toss everything together. The cabbage will wilt with the steam created.

Uncover the paella and, using a large spoon, make a small well at the side of the paella and put a spoonful of cabbage in. Repeat this around the edge of the paella until there are lots of small cabbage stations.

Serve with lemon wedges.

Pumpkin and Filo Parcels with Sweet Red Pepper Sauce 86

Pasta Primavera 88

Linguine with Tomato and Mozzarella 90

Spinach and Ricotta Gnocchi with Tomato Sauce 92

Falafel Burgers with Tahini and Lemon Sauce 94

Lentil and Sweet Potato Burgers with Yellow Pepper Sauce 96

Borlotti Bean and Vegetable Stew 98

Summer Vegetable Pilaf with Yoghurt Sauce 100

Cassoulet of Summer Vegetables 102

Courgette and Herb Bake 104

Pindi Channa 106

Leek and Butterbean Gratin 108

Poor Man's Potatoes 110

Spicy Lentils with Grilled Halloumi Cheese 112

Thai Yellow Curry with Peanut Salsa 114

Vegetarian Moussaka 116

Rocket and Pumpkin Seed Pesto 118

Pumpkin and Filo Parcels with Sweet Red Pepper Sauce

A great meal for entertaining, this began as a Christmas dinner recipe as it works a treat for vegetarians alongside the traditional dinner. We all enjoyed it so much that it pops up when we are cooking for friends or family. Everything can be prepared earlier and put aside until you are ready for dinner.

500g firm pumpkin or butternut squash flesh
500g red onions
150g feta cheese
handful coriander
75g butter
filo pastry
olive oil
salt and black pepper

Red Pepper Sauce
1 onion
2 red peppers
25g butter
125ml glass white wine
100ml vegetable stock
salt and black pepper

Serves 4–6

Preheat the oven to 180°C (350°F), Gas Mark 4.

Peel the pumpkin and chop into 2cm chunks. Toss in a little olive oil and season with salt and pepper. Put on a baking tray and roast in the oven for 20–25 minutes until cooked through.

Peel the onions, cut in half, and then slice thinly. Heat a frying pan and add a little olive oil, then the onions. When the onions begin to sizzle steadily, turn the heat down a bit. Season with a pinch of salt, then cook slowly for 25–30 minutes. Stir frequently. If the onions begin to stick or brown, turn the heat further down. The onions should slowly melt and sweeten. When the onions are cooked, tip into a bowl with the cooked pumpkin.

Crumble the feta on top, add the coriander leaves and stalks, chopped, and toss everything together. Season to taste with salt and pepper.

Melt the butter in a small pan. Carefully unroll the filo pastry and lay one sheet on the work surface. Brush with melted butter then fold in half or put another sheet on top and brush with butter. Whether you fold the pastry in half or use two sheets will depend on which brand of filo you are using. The Greek and Turkish versions are usually larger at 30 x 50cm and so can be folded in half. Turn over, so the butter side is down, and put a small pile of the pumpkin mix in the middle. Take the four corners of the filo and carefully scrunch up into a parcel and put on a baking tray. Assemble 3 more parcels. Bake in the oven for about 20 minutes.

For the sauce: peel and chop the onion, and deseed and chop the peppers.

Melt the butter in a small pan, add the onions and cook until they melt down a little. Add the chopped peppers and cook for a few minutes. Pour over the white wine and enough vegetable stock to just cover the vegetables. Bring to the boil, then lower the heat to simmer for 20–25 minutes, until the peppers are tender.

Take off the heat and buzz to a smooth purée. Season with salt and pepper and add more stock if it's too thick.

To serve, spread a puddle of the sauce on a plate and place the parcel on top.

Pasta Primavera

This is a great dish for early summer when the intense flavours of new season vegetables can be showcased. It's very flexible, so you can use whatever you can get your hands on. Try to find a selection of three or four vegetables such as broad beans, peas, asparagus and courgettes. Be sure to buy small courgettes, as when they get big they are essentially water balls and, although they look good, the flavour is pretty diluted. Sometimes I make the recipe with cream, and at other times with a little pesto and olive oil. This is the dairy version. If you want to make the pesto version add 2 tablespoons of pesto and a spoonful of pasta cooking water to the vegetables at the same time as draining the pasta. (See rocket pesto recipe page 118) The trick is to cook each vegetable quickly and in the order of time that it takes each to cook, and to coordinate cooking the pasta so the sauce and pasta are ready at the same time.

150g podded broad beans
1 bunch asparagus
1–2 small courgettes
1 small new season onion
25g butter
25ml olive oil
250ml cream
150g peas, fresh or frozen
50g Parmesan, grated
salt and black pepper
pasta, fresh or dried
handful parsley, chopped

Serves 4–6

Put a large pot of salted water on to boil for the pasta and another one for blanching the beans.

When the water is boiling add the broad beans to the pot without salt. Cook them for 3-4 minutes, depending on how big they are, and then drain and refresh in cold water.

Snap the woody end from the asparagus and chop the stem in centimetre pieces saving the last 9-10cm at the spear end. Cut the courgettes in quarters lengthwise and then into approx. 1cm cubes. Peel and chop the onion.

From now, the sauce will take 10-12 minutes to make, so time the pasta accordingly. Follow the instructions on the packet and drain when ready.

Heat a frying pan and add the butter and oil. Add the chopped onion to the hot pan and cook for a minute. Stir the asparagus stems into the onions and cook for a couple of minutes more before adding the chopped courgette and asparagus tips. Season with salt and black pepper, then cook on a high heat for a few minutes.

Add the cream, peas and cooked broad beans. Bring to the boil and let the sauce bubble up to reduce, then stir in the Parmesan. Check for seasoning.

Toss the pasta together with the sauce and serve immediately with a little chopped parsley and grated Parmesan.

Linguine with Tomato and Mozzarella

This is a quick and extremely tasty recipe which doesn't require any fancy equipment or make much washing up: a large saucepan to cook the linguine and a small saucepan for the sauce and you're away. Please don't be put off trying this recipe by the mention of the anchovies as this isn't a fishy dish.
In this instance the anchovies are acting as a flavour enhancer and, once cooked in the sauce, add an extra dimension while dissolving completely. We prefer to use buffalo mozzarella as it is creamier than the regular mozzarella but both types will work in this recipe. Good quality pasta such as De Cecco will make all the difference. If you can't get your hands on linguine, use spaghetti instead.

2–3 large cloves garlic
1–2 red chillies
75ml olive oil
4–5 anchovy fillets
2 x 400g tins tomatoes
2 x 125g balls fresh mozzarella
bunch basil
500g linguine
salt and black pepper

Serves 4

Peel and finely chop the garlic and chop the chillies (a good pinch of chilli flakes would work well here too).

Put a frying pan on the heat with 50ml (about 2 tbsp) of the olive oil. Add the garlic and chilli. Don't allow the oil to get too hot as garlic burns easily and will spoil the sauce. Cook gently for a minute or so.

Stir in the anchovies. As they heat, mash the anchovies with a wooden spoon.

Chop the tomatoes and add. Season with salt and pepper.

Bring this tomato sauce to the boil, then turn down and simmer for about 20 minutes. When the oil comes to the surface, the sauce is ready.

Dice the mozzarella into 1cm pieces, chop the basil and put both into a bowl. Season with salt, black pepper and drizzle with olive oil. Mix together gently and leave aside for the flavours to infuse.

Bring a big pot of water to the boil, add a tablespoon of salt and cook the linguine according to the directions on the packet – usually about 11 minutes. Drain and put into a warm bowl; I warm the bowl by straining the pasta water onto it – a little energy conservation.

Pour the tomato sauce over the linguine and scatter with the mozzarella.

Spinach and Ricotta Gnocchi with Tomato Sauce

Gnocchi, pronounced noki/njoki, are little Italian dumplings. They are usually made with potatoes, but there are lots of regional variations. This recipe is for gnocchi malfatti (which has a lovely ring to it) and means badly formed. These gnocchi are like little bon-bons made of ricotta and they melt in the mouth. The secret to success in cooking these is the temperature of the water. A rolling boil will disintegrate these delicate little dumplings so bring a pot of water to the boil then turn to the lowest simmer before slipping them in.

250g spinach
250g ricotta cheese
2 large eggs
100g Parmesan cheese, grated
3 tbsp fine semolina
nutmeg
salt and black pepper

Tomato Sauce
1 small onion, quartered
2 x 400g tins tomatoes
50g butter
handful fresh basil leaves
salt and black pepper

Serves 4

For the tomato sauce, put the onion, tomatoes and butter into a saucepan, season with salt and pepper, and bring to the boil. Turn the heat down to simmer and cook, uncovered, for a good 30 minutes. The tomatoes become sweeter and richer with the cooking. Buzz the sauce until smooth and check the seasoning. Chop the basil leaves and stir in.

This may be a little too much sauce for the gnocchi but the remainder can be kept in the fridge for 3–4 days. It's kind of a universal tomato sauce and has numerous uses: we use it for pasta, pizza, toasted bread, stews and anything that needs to sit in a little sauce.

Bring a large pot of water to the boil. Wash the spinach and take out any extra thick stems. Add a heaped teaspoon of salt to the boiling water and drop in the spinach. Make sure the spinach is completely immersed. When the water returns to the boil cook the spinach for 1 minute, then drain and plunge into a bowl of cold water. This will stop the spinach from cooking further. Drain and squeeze it in your hands to remove the excess water. Finely chop the spinach and squeeze again.

Put the ricotta into a bowl and beat together with the eggs until creamy.

Stir in the spinach, grated cheese and semolina, then season with a little grated nutmeg and some salt and pepper.

Bring a large pot of salted water to the boil, and turn down to the lowest simmer. Warm a serving bowl in the oven ready to put the gnocchi into to keep them warm.

Wet your hands and form small balls with the gnocchi mixture. Gently slip them into the water. When the gnocchi rise back to the surface they are cooked. Remove with a slotted spoon and put onto the warm serving dish to stop them from cooling too quickly.

Dress with the tomato and basil sauce or olive oil and fresh herbs and serve immediately.

Falafel Burgers with Tahini and Lemon Sauce

One of our first million dollar ideas was a takeaway food van, which we drove around to all the music festivals in the summer. It was a Ford parcel van, which we converted and emblazoned with the words 'International Takeaways' in rainbow colours across the front. The radiator was fluorescent pink and looked like something in Roddy Doyle's book The Van. We made falafels which we served in pitta breads with salad and tahini sauce. We used to soak the chickpeas overnight and grind them up in a manual grain mill (a bit like an old-fashioned meat mincer, which was clamped to the counter). The grill for the pitta breads was jerry-rigged out of an old storage heater and lava rock that we brought home from Sicily. We were a bit premature with this adventure. Most people didn't know what a chickpea was, let alone a falafel, but we had a lot of fun. The recipe that we used has evolved over the years and right now we are making the falafels in a burger shape which can be shallow fried so it's easier and healthier.

200g dried chickpeas
1 x 400g tin chickpeas
1 large onion
3–4 cloves garlic
1 tsp salt
1 tbsp ground cumin
large handful coriander, chopped
large handful parsley, chopped
2–3 tbsp gram or plain flour
olive oil

Tahini and Lemon Sauce
3 tbsp light tahini
1–2 cloves garlic, peeled and chopped
juice 1 lemon
water
salt

Serves 4–6

For the tahini sauce, put the tahini, garlic and lemon juice into a small bowl and mix together. It will become very thick. Thin with enough water to make a thick pouring sauce. Season to taste with a little salt.

Soak the dried chickpeas in cold water overnight. The next day, drain them and put them, uncooked, into a food processor and blitz until finely ground.

Drain the tin of chickpeas and rinse them under the tap.

Peel and finely chop the onion and garlic. Heat a small frying pan, add a little olive oil and fry the onions for 2–3 minutes then stir in the chopped garlic and fry for 1 minute longer.

Tip the onions and garlic into the ground chickpeas in the food processor together with the tinned chickpeas, salt, ground cumin and chopped herbs.

Blitz everything until fairly smooth. Tip into a bowl and sieve in 2 tbsp of the gram flour and mix well. We use gram flour as it is gluten-free, but any flour will work.

Heat a large frying pan and pour in enough oil to cover the bottom. Wet your hands and form the mix into small burgers – not too thick – and slip them into the pan. If the mix is too wet to stay together, add a little more gram flour and try again. Flip them over and fry the other side.

We serve these at home in toasted pitta bread with shredded lettuce and tomato at the bottom, a burger or two on top, drizzled with the tahini sauce.

Lentil and Sweet Potato Burgers with Yellow Pepper Sauce

We make burgers of some kind or another every day in our shop. Sometimes they have quinoa, millet or brown rice, and sometimes we throw in lentils or beans. Although the key ingredients might vary, there is always a good ratio of sautéed vegetables and herbs in the mix. On a domestic level these burgers are a good home for leftovers and as long as you follow the basic recipe you can be quite creative. The following recipe starts from scratch but feel free to swop the ingredients about. Whatever you choose, chop the vegetables up pretty small or the burgers won't stay together and don't omit the potato flour as this is the glue. The tasty yellow pepper sauce is very fast to make. I also love the colour – it makes the burgers look pretty funky on the plate.

100g Puy lentils
200g millet
2 onions
2–3 stalks celery
1 large sweet potato
2 tbsp olive oil
2 cloves garlic
1 tsp garam masala
soy sauce or tamari
handful coriander or parsley
2–3 tbsp potato flour
salt and black pepper
oil for frying – vegetable, sunflower

Yellow Pepper Sauce
1 onion
25g butter or olive oil
2 yellow peppers
200ml vegetable stock
125ml white wine
4 cardamom pods
1 star anise
lemon juice
salt and pepper

Makes 8 burgers

First, make the pepper sauce. Peel and chop the onion. Heat the butter or oil in a small saucepan and add the onions. Keep them cooking on a moderate heat while you chop the peppers. Add the peppers and cook them for a few minutes before stirring in the vegetable stock, white wine, cardamoms and star anise. Bring to the boil then simmer for about 20-25 minutes until the pepper is cooked. Remove the cardamoms and star anise and liquidise the sauce to a smooth purée. Season with salt and pepper. If you think the sauce needs a lift add a squeeze of lemon juice.

Put the lentils into a saucepan with about 300ml cold water. Bring to the boil, cover with a lid, and simmer for 20 minutes. The lentils should be just cooked. Drain and rinse.

Put the millet into another saucepan and stir on medium heat for a few minutes until beginning to toast. Carefully add 300ml water – it will splatter as the pan is hot. Add a little salt and bring to the boil, cover with a lid and simmer for 12 minutes. Take the pot off the heat and leave it to relax with the lid on for 10 minutes before fluffing up with a fork. Keep the lid off and leave to cool.

Peel and finely chop the onions. Chop the celery into 1cm dice. Peel the sweet potato and cut into slices, cut the slices into strips, then cut the strips into 1cm dice.

Heat a large frying pan and add the olive oil and vegetables. Keep the heat high until they are constantly sizzling, then turn the heat to medium. Season with salt and pepper and stir every couple of minutes for about 10 minutes.

Peel and chop the garlic and add to the vegetables. Cook for 5 minutes more. Stir in the garam masala.

Tip the drained lentils, millet and vegetables into a large bowl. Season with soy sauce or tamari, salt and pepper to taste.

Chop the coriander or parsley with their stalks and stir in. Add 2 tbsp of the potato flour and mix well.

Wet your hands to stop the mix from sticking to you. Take a handful of the mix and form a ball by squishing it together. If the mixture is crumbly and falls apart, add more potato flour and try again. Flatten each ball into a burger shape.

Heat a frying pan, add enough oil to just cover the bottom and gently fry the burgers. Don't poke them about. Let a golden crust form on the bottom before turning over and cooking the other side.

Pour a little puddle of the yellow pepper sauce on each plate and sit a burger on top. Garnish with chopped coriander or parsley.

Borlotti Bean and Vegetable Stew

This is a summer dish, quite like a minestrone, which uses a type of bean that has become popular in recent times called borlotti. I started growing borlotti beans a few years back and it is now becoming an addiction. They don't do very well outside in the Irish climate but they thrive inside the tunnel. Fresh borlottis are quite a revelation. As they ripen the pods turn a brilliant pink and the beans inside are marbled pink and cream in colour. They cook up plump and velvety, a mile nicer than dried and reconstituted beans which are starchy in comparison. If you can't find fresh you can use dried or tinned beans. Cannellini make a good substitute: soak them overnight and follow the cooking instructions below but extend the cooking time to about one hour.

Beans
250g podded borlotti beans
1 small onion, quartered
2 cloves garlic, peeled
1 large tomato, chopped
sprig fresh sage
salt and black pepper

Vegetable Base
1–2 onions
2 stalks celery
75–100ml olive oil
Parmesan rind (optional)
2–3 bulbs fennel
2–3 carrots
3–4 waxy potatoes
2 cloves garlic
3 large, plump tomatoes
125ml white wine
700ml vegetable stock or water
2 small courgettes
handful basil leaves
salt and black pepper

Serves 4–6

Put all the ingredients for the beans in a small saucepan and cover with water. Bring to the boil, cover with a lid and cook for about 30 minutes, until the beans are just tender. Remove the lid and raise the heat to high. Cook until the liquid has reduced by about half, then season with salt and pepper. Stir in a good glug of tasty olive oil and keep until needed.

Peel and chop the onion and chop the celery into 1cm dice. Heat a large saucepan and add a good glug of olive oil to generously coat the bottom. Add the onion and celery and season with a little salt. If using Parmesan rind add it now. Keep cooking on a medium-high heat. You should be able to hear the vegetables sizzling away.

Prepare and slowly add the rest of the vegetables in the following order: quarter the fennel lengthwise; peel and chop the carrots and potatoes into about 3cm chunks; peel and chop the garlic; roughly chop the tomatoes.

Allow to bubble gently for 20 minutes.

Season with salt and black pepper.

Add the white wine, let it bubble up, then add the stock. Cook for about 10 minutes.

Cut the courgettes into quarters lengthwise and chop into 2cm chunks. In a frying pan heat about 1 tbsp oil to coat the bottom and add the courgettes. Give them a good shake, then season with salt and black pepper. Stir on high heat for a few minutes, then tip into the pot of vegetables. Cook for a few more minutes, then take off the heat and stir in the basil.

Serve the stew in a bowl with the borlotti beans piled in the middle.

Summer Vegetable Pilaf with Yoghurt Sauce

Pilaf is a Middle Eastern rice dish, gently spiced and cooked, in this instance, with vegetables and stock. It has a wonderful fresh flavour and is the perfect home for whatever young summer vegetables you may have to hand. I have used broad beans, peas and asparagus, but this recipe is very flexible. Later in the summer I add courgettes and fennel. It really is up to you: use whatever you fancy in the vegetable department and follow the basic recipe. The same rule applies to the herbs: fresh mint, coriander, parsley, dill or fennel are all delicious. This can be eaten as a dish in itself or alongside grilled meat or fish. If you don't grow broad beans, look for them at farmers' markets; easy enough to cultivate, they are popular with the organic growers.

300g basmati rice
250g fresh asparagus
2–3 onions
75g butter or 75ml olive oil
1 tsp fennel seeds
4–5cm cinnamon stick
10 allspice berries
450ml vegetable stock
250g broad beans, podded
150g peas, fresh or frozen
large handful fresh herbs

Yoghurt Sauce
1 clove garlic, chopped
200ml Greek yoghurt
50ml extra virgin olive oil
salt

Serves 4–6

For the yoghurt sauce, mix together the garlic and yoghurt, then whisk in the olive oil and season with salt.

Cover the basmati with warm water and put aside.

Trim the asparagus. Chop off the tougher end of the stems and set aside. Chop the rest of the stem into 1cm pieces except for the top 10cm spear.

Peel and chop the onions.

Melt the butter or heat the oil gently in a saucepan with a tight-fitting lid. Add the fennel seeds, cinnamon stick and allspice berries to the butter/oil and cook gently, covered, for a couple of minutes.

Stir in the onions and pieces of chopped asparagus stems. Season with a little salt. Cook until softened, but don't let them brown.

Rinse the rice in a sieve under a running tap, shake off the excess water, then stir into the onions. Cook for 1 minute.

Add the stock and bring to the boil.

Stir in the broad beans, peas and asparagus spears. Taste and add more salt if you think it needs it, then turn the heat down and cover with the lid. Cook on a low heat for 5 minutes, then turn down to the lowest simmer and cook for a further 5 minutes. Turn the heat off but don't open the lid, just leave the pilaf to relax for a further 5-10 minutes.

Just before serving, stir the chopped herbs (chopped mint/fennel/parsley/coriander or a combination of all) into the rice and heap on a plate. Spoon the yoghurt sauce on top.

Cassoulet of Summer Vegetables

This is a vegetarian version of the French dish, cassoulet. Traditionally it is made with duck and pork, topped with toasted breadcrumbs and baked in a casserole, hence the name. We've swapped the duck and pork for aubergines and courgettes and further changed the recipe by using bashed-up tortilla chips for the topping – a very handy alternative to bread, making it suitable for coeliacs.

300g dried butterbeans or 2 x 400g tins
1 aubergine
2 onions
2 stalks celery
1 bay leaf
3 peppers, any colour
3 plump cloves garlic
½ bottle white wine
800g fresh or tinned tomatoes
3 courgettes
handful fresh basil

100g tortilla chips
1 clove garlic
handful parsley
125g cheddar, grated
olive oil
salt and pepper

Serves 4–6

If you are using dried butterbeans soak them overnight in plenty of cold water. For tinned beans, simply drain and rinse before use. Put them in a saucepan the next day, making sure the water level comes up at least 2cm above the beans and bring to the boil. Turn down to a simmer and put the lid on. Do not add salt. Cook for 40–60 minutes until the beans are tender but still keep their shape. Drain and put aside.

Wash and cut the aubergine into quarters lengthwise, then chop into 1cm chunks. Sprinkle over a little salt and toss well. Put in a bowl and leave to sweat.

Peel and chop the onions and celery into 1cm dice. Heat a large saucepan and add a couple of tablespoons of olive oil, the onions, celery and bay leaf. Cook on a high heat until sizzling, then season with a little salt and turn the heat to medium.

Wash and de-seed the peppers and cut into about 3cm chunks. Add to the onion/celery mix. Continue cooking until they soften. Peel and chop three of the garlic cloves and stir in. Cook for a further few minutes.

Pour in the wine. Allow to bubble up so that the alcohol evaporates, then stir in the tomatoes and cooked butterbeans. Bring to the boil and season with some salt and pepper. Leave to simmer for 15–20 minutes.

Meanwhile preheat the oven to 180°C (350°F), Gas Mark 4.

Wash the courgettes and cut into 1cm thick slices.

Squeeze the chopped aubergine chunks in your hands to remove excess water.

Heat a large frying pan, add some olive oil and fry the courgettes and aubergines in batches until they are lightly browned. Don't overcrowd the pan.

Tip them into the saucepan with the rest of the vegetables and stir. Take off the heat, check the seasoning and stir in some chopped basil. Pour the whole mix into a large ovenproof dish.

Deflate the bag of tortilla chips and bash with a rolling pin or wooden spoon until they become crumbs. Peel and chop one garlic clove and the parsley, then mix with the bashed tortilla chips and grated cheddar. Sprinkle over the top of the vegetable mixture.

Bake in the oven for 30–40 minutes, until the sauce is bubbling at the edges and the crust is golden.

Serve with a green salad and some spuds or crusty bread.

Courgette and Herb Bake

This is our take on an old Turkish dish called firinda kabak which we enjoy when the courgettes are in full swing. We have tweaked the recipe over the years and this version uses polenta instead of flour. This gives it an interesting texture and makes it suitable for coeliacs and people with wheat intolerance. Small courgettes give the best flavour.

6 small courgettes
6 spring onions
generous handful mint
generous handful dill or fennel
generous handful parsley
75g Gruyère, Comté or Emmental cheese

3 large eggs
75g feta cheese
100g polenta
12 black olives
50g butter
salt and black pepper

Serves 4–6

Preheat the oven to 180°C (350°F), Gas Mark 4.

Line a 9 inch/23cm square tin or baking dish with parchment paper.

Grate the courgettes coarsely, put into a bowl and toss with a little salt. Leave for 10 minutes then gather into your hands and squeeze gently to extract the excess water. Place in a clean bowl.

Clean and chop the spring onion. Chop the mint, dill and parsley. Grate the Gruyère cheese and mix in a bowl with courgettes, eggs, herbs and spring onion. Add most of the feta, reserving some for the top. Mix well, then add the polenta and season with salt and pepper. Pour the mix into the prepared tin or dish.

Scatter the olives on top, the remaining feta and dot with little pieces of the butter.

Bake for about 45 minutes or until golden on top.

Cut into squares and serve hot or cold.

Pindi Channa

I first ate this chickpea and pomegranate dish sitting on a rooftop restaurant in Jodphur in Rajasthan, India. I was blown away by the fresh, sweet explosions of the jewelled pomegranate seeds glistening on top of the chickpea dal. It looked amazing and certainly elevated what is a rather pedestrian looking dish into something quite exotic. The chickpeas are cooked with tamarind which give a lovely, sour twist and is the perfect complement to the pomegranate.

1 tsp tamarind concentrate
100ml hot water
1 heaped tsp cumin seeds
250g onions
5–6 cloves garlic
25g fresh ginger
1–2 chillies
25ml vegetable oil
1 tsp turmeric
1 x 400g tin tomatoes
500g cooked chickpeas (see page 80) or 2 x 400g tins
1 heaped tsp garam masala
1 pomegranate
handful fresh coriander

Serves 4–6

Put the tamarind into the hot water and stir until dissolved.

Put a small frying pan on the heat and gently toast the cumin seeds until they lightly brown and become aromatic. Put aside to cool.

Peel and chop the onions, garlic, ginger and chillies.

Heat a saucepan and add the vegetable oil. Add the onions, season with a little salt and cook without browning for about 10 minutes.

Stir in the chopped garlic, ginger and chilli. Cook gently for a few minutes, then stir in the turmeric. Chop the tomatoes and add with the toasted cumin seeds and tamarind juice.

Add the chickpeas to the sauce in the pan. If using tinned chickpeas, rinse and drain them before adding.

Mix everything together and cook for 15 minutes. Just before serving, stir in the garam masala and add more salt if needed.

Roll the pomegranate around on the table or on a chopping board, using a little pressure with the palm of the hand to loosen the seeds. Cut it in half and tip the seeds out into a sieve; remove any bits of membrane and drain off any excess juice – you can drink the juice later.

Serve the chickpea dal with the pomegranate seeds and chopped coriander on top. Eat it with basmati rice and thinly sliced tomato and red onions, seasoned with a little salt and lemon juice. Some thick creamy yoghurt on the side is also good.

Leek and Butterbean Gratin

Gratin simply means a dish cooked in the oven or under the grill to achieve a crispy top. It's usually, but not always, strewn with breadcrumbs and cheese. It's real, old-fashioned comfort food. The breadcrumb and cheese element of this recipe is optional but if you have the time and inclination it will add an extra dimension to the dish. The sauce can also be poured over the vegetables and baked without the crumbs. Tins of beans are handy for this recipe, just drain and rinse them before using.

2–3 leeks
100ml milk
200g mushrooms
25g butter
300g cooked butterbeans
salt and pepper

Cheese Sauce
300ml milk
30g butter
30g flour
100g cheddar, grated
soy sauce

Topping
100g fresh breadcrumbs
30g cheese, grated

Serves 4–6

Preheat the oven to 180°C (350°F), Gas Mark 4.

Trim the leeks and rinse under the tap to remove any grit, then chop into 1cm slices. Place in a saucepan with the milk and a little salt and pepper. Bring to the boil, cover with a lid, and then simmer until tender for 10–15 minutes. Drain the leeks, reserving the milk.

Slice the mushrooms. Melt the butter in a frying pan and add the mushrooms. Season with a little salt and pepper, toss well and cook on a high heat for a few minutes.

Gently mix the leeks and butterbeans together and put into an ovenproof dish. Scatter the mushrooms on top.

Now for the cheese sauce. Heat the milk together with the milk reserved from cooking the leeks.

Melt the butter in a separate saucepan. Stir in the flour and cook gently for a couple of minutes, then whisk in the heated milk. Add the grated cheese, soy sauce and season with salt and pepper.

Pour the sauce over the vegetables, giving them a little poke to mix.

Toss the breadcrumbs and grated cheese together and scatter over the dish.

Bake for about 30 minutes, until golden on top and bubbling around the edges. Serve with green vegetables such as stir-fried cabbage, broccoli or salad leaves, and spuds.

Poor Man's Potatoes

This dish originated in Spain where it is known as patatas a lo pobre. It's a simple dish made in a frying pan or skillet. In Spain, peppers, potatoes and onions are staples and every house has olive oil and garlic, but the vital ingredient for this recipe is patience. The onions, peppers and garlic sweeten with the slow cooking and the potatoes have a great flavour when cooked gently in olive oil. So peel the vegetables, get the pan sizzling and park yourself somewhere comfortable close to the cooker with the newspaper and give the pan a regular stir. We like to eat this with a fried egg on top but it is also delicious accompanied by sausages, black pudding or grilled meat.

3 onions
150ml olive oil
2–3 peppers
2 bay leaves
1 kg waxy potatoes
3–4 cloves garlic
salt and pepper
balsamic/red wine vinegar

Serves 4–6

Peel the onions, cut into half and slice thinly. Heat the frying pan or skillet, add half the olive oil and the onions. Season with a little salt and when the onions are sizzling, turn the heat down to a moderate simmer for about 15 minutes.

Wash the peppers, remove the seeds and cut into 1cm strips, then stir into the onions together with the bay leaves. Cook gently for 10 minutes.

Peel the potatoes and cut into quarters, then chop into small chunks, adding to the pan as you go. Add the remaining olive oil.

Peel the garlic, cut into quarters and stir in. Season with salt and pepper.

Cook for about 30 minutes, or until the potatoes are tender, giving regular stirs so nothing sticks to the pan.

Serve with a drizzle of vinegar, using the best quality you can afford.

Spicy Lentils with Grilled Halloumi Cheese

This is an easy, warming lentil recipe. It's one we've been making for years which originated in the Quaglino cookbook. It was only when I watched Con make it for dinner one night that I realised I don't follow the recipe at all. I thought he had some fancy pants angle on it when in fact he was following the recipe and I had moved on to my own version. It doesn't seem to make much difference though, as both versions are equally delicious. Our current favourite way to eat this dish is with halloumi cheese, which we grill and pile on top. Here's my recipe.

2–3 red onions
3 cloves garlic
3cm ginger
2 red chillies
50g butter
4 cardamom pods
2 star anise
1 tsp dried turmeric
3–4 tomatoes, chopped
300g Puy lentils
600ml vegetable stock
handful fresh coriander
1–2 tbsp Thai fish sauce
100ml cream
300g halloumi cheese
olive oil
black pepper

Serves 4–6

Peel and chop the onions. Peel and chop the garlic and ginger and finely chop the chilli.

Heat a saucepan, add the butter (or 50ml olive oil) and the onions. Cook on a medium heat, stirring from time to time until the onions begin to melt down a little. Add the garlic, ginger and chilli and cook for a couple of minutes, then stir in the cardamom, star anise and turmeric.

Chop the tomatoes and add to the pan. Keep cooking until the tomatoes begin to break down, then add the lentils and stock. Bring to the boil, then cover with a lid and simmer for about 40 minutes or until the lentils are tender.

Chop the coriander, including the stalks.

Season the lentils with the fish sauce then stir in the cream and most of the coriander.

Cut the halloumi into slices, season with black pepper and rub with a few drops of olive oil. Be mean with the olive oil, you don't need much. Put on a grill pan or grill, then cook the halloumi until golden.

To serve, put a ladleful of lentils onto each plate, place the grilled halloumi on top and finish with the remaining coriander.

Thai Yellow Curry with Peanut Salsa

I love Thai curries but really and truly the reason I love this recipe is because of the peanut salsa. I learned how to make this recipe when I was in Chiang Mai in the north of Thailand where it was made with chicken and potatoes. We pounded the paste in a mortar and pestle and it tasted great, but for quick, everyday eating I use a good ready-made Thai paste. This is a really easy dish to throw together and it's the only Thai curry that doesn't contain any shrimp paste or fish sauce, so it's ideal for a vegetarian version. The peanut salsa does push the boat out a bit on the effort front but it's well worth it. Be sure to roast the peanuts until they are light brown – they taste more peanutty that way. A real Thai curry is always made to order for one or two people, so I cook it in stages. This way I can cook a bigger amount, put it all together at the end and the vegetables aren't overcooked.

600g pumpkin or butternut squash
1 red onion
1 red pepper
150g mangetout peas
3–4 cloves garlic
250g tofu
1 heaped tbsp Thai yellow curry paste
2 x 400ml tins coconut milk
1 dssp palm or light muscovado sugar
large pinch ground turmeric
1 tbsp soy sauce or tamari
oil (vegetable, sunflower or rapeseed)

Peanut Salsa
3 tbsp granulated sugar
3 tbsp water
2 tbsp vinegar – rice, cider, white wine
75g peanuts
1 small red onion
20cm cucumber
1–2 chillies (optional)
handful coriander, chopped

Serves 4–6

For the peanut salsa, put the sugar and water into a small saucepan and bring to the boil. As it heats it will become less cloudy and eventually clear. As soon as this happens, take it off the heat and leave to cool. Stir in the vinegar and set aside.

Roast the peanuts in a dry pan or in the oven. When the skins are easy to rub off and the peanuts are golden, take them off the heat and put onto a clean tea-towel. Gather the tea-towel together and rub vigorously to remove the skins. Separate the peanuts from the skins by picking them out or taking the peanuts outside and giving them a good huff and puff to blow the skins away. Put the skinned peanuts into a food processor or use a mortar and pestle. If using a processor use the pulse button to avoid over grinding.

Peel and finely chop the onion. Quarter the cucumber lengthways and cut off the seeds. Chop to a small dice. Chop the chillies and add to the syrup with the cucumber and onion.

When you're ready to serve, add the peanuts and mix everything together, finishing with the coriander.

Preheat the oven to 180°C (350°F), Gas Mark 4.

Peel the pumpkin and remove the seeds. Chop into chunks of about 2cm and put on a baking tray. Toss lightly with a little oil. Roast in the oven for about 20 minutes or until the pumpkin is just tender.

Peel the onion and cut into little wedges lengthwise. Wash the pepper, cut in half and remove the seeds then thinly slice. Top and tail the mangetout. Peel and chop the garlic. Chop the tofu into 1cm cubes.

Heat a little oil in a wok or large frying pan, then add the onion wedges and red pepper. Cook on a high heat for 3–4 minutes, then throw in the mangetout and garlic. Toss everything together and cook for a couple of minutes longer, then tip into a bowl and set aside.

Add a little more oil to the pan and stir in the curry paste. Cook on a medium heat for a couple of minutes – don't let it burn – then stir in the coconut milk. Add the palm sugar, turmeric, soy sauce and tofu. When everything comes to the boil, tip in the roasted pumpkin and fried vegetables and gently mix everything together.

Serve with basmati rice and a good dollop of the peanut salsa on top.

Vegetarian Moussaka

One of my first culinary adventures was to make a moussaka in a domestic science class at school. It's a Greek dish of minced lamb and aubergines. I hadn't a clue what I was doing but I was curious as it sounded so exotic. My mum scoured the town for aubergines, which were relatively uncommon at that time, and I carted all the ingredients into school on a bus. The instructions must have said something like 'fry the aubergine in oil' which I did, pouring in more oil as the aubergine drank it up like a sponge. The resulting dish was a disgusting, sodden mass, and nobody wanted to eat it. I have since learned to salt the aubergines, not so much to eliminate any bitterness, but to slow down the oil absorption. And for a dish like moussaka I now brush the aubergines with oil and roast them in the oven rather than frying in the pan. Aubergines cooked this way have a wonderful velvety 'meatiness' which, paired with Puy lentils, makes a great vegetarian dish.

125g Puy lentils
1 bay leaf
2–3 aubergines
1–2 onions
2 sticks celery
2–3 cloves garlic, peeled and chopped
2 x 400 tins tomatoes
fresh basil or oregano

225g ricotta cheese
3 large eggs
250ml cream
75g grated Parmesan cheese
olive oil
salt and pepper

Put the lentils into a saucepan and cover them with water. Add the bay leaf and bring to the boil. Turn down to simmer, cover with a lid and cook for 15–20 minutes until the lentils are tender. Drain off any remaining liquid and discard the bay leaf.

Slice the aubergines lengthwise, a little less than a centimetre thick – not too skinny as they'll shrink slightly while cooking. Sprinkle with a little salt and leave them to sweat in a bowl for about 30 minutes.

Preheat oven to 180°C (350°F), Gas Mark 4.

Dab the liquid that accumulates on the aubergines with kitchen paper or a clean tea towel to dry them off. Brush olive oil onto a large oven tray and fill with the aubergines. Brush the tops of the aubergines with olive oil. Bake in the oven for 15–20 minutes. The aubergines should be soft, not crispy.

Peel and chop the onion, chop the celery and sauté together in a little olive oil. When they are soft and translucent add the chopped garlic and cook for a couple of minutes longer. Add the tomatoes and cook for about 30 minutes. Take off the heat.

Stir in the drained lentils and season with salt and pepper. Add the chopped basil or oregano.

In a bowl mash the ricotta together with the eggs and beat in the cream. Stir in the grated Parmesan and season.

To assemble the moussaka pour a third of the tomato lentil mix into an ovenproof dish. Use half the baked aubergines to form a layer on top. Add a third more of the tomato lentil mix, another layer of aubergines and then the remaining lentil mix. Pour the egg mix over and bake in the oven for approx. 25 minutes until the topping has risen and is golden.

Serve with a green salad.

Rocket and Pumpkin Seed Pesto

Rocket, true to its name, shoots up; it's an almost foolproof introduction to vegetable growing. Sow the seeds directly into a seed bed, window box or patio container. Five or six days later you will discover lots of tiny rocket plants emerging. Within three to four weeks you will be harvesting your own rocket and you won't need to buy skimpy little plastic packs of rocket from the supermarket anymore! It's a pick-and-come-again plant. Like all salads and herbs, rocket likes to be picked regularly or it will think its job is done and go to seed. However, if you want a constant supply for the summer season you will need to sow the seeds again. We sow every six weeks or so. The delicious peppery leaves can be used alone or with a combination of salad leaves. Simply toss with a little vinaigrette. They also make a superb pesto.

25g pumpkin seeds
25g pine nuts
1–2 cloves garlic
150g rocket
150ml olive oil
juice ½ lemon
50g Parmesan cheese
salt

Heat a frying pan and gently toast the pumpkin seeds. Place them in a food processor with the pine nuts and garlic, and blitz until fairly finely ground. Add the rocket and, with the motor running, slowly pour in the olive oil and lemon juice. Add the Parmesan and mix well.

Season with a little salt and adjust the consistency by adding a little more oil if necessary. Tip into a bowl. Put a layer of olive oil over the top if the pesto isn't going to be used immediately. This will stop it from oxidising. Use within the week.

To serve with pasta, cook the pasta then take a couple of tablespoons of the cooking water and mix with the pesto to make a sauce then toss together with the pasta. Finish with shavings of parmesan and rocket leaves.

Courgette, Tomato, Basil and Mozzarella Tart 122

Kale, Gorgonzola and Pumpkin Tart 124

Pissaladière Tart 126

Roasted Beetroot, Rainbow Chard and Chèvre Tart 128

Spinach, Sweet Potato and Comté Tart 130

Savoury Pastry 132

Savoury Tarts

Courgette, Tomato, Basil and Mozzarella Tart

Anyone who grows courgettes will know that once they start coming there's no stopping them. Picked small they have plenty of flavour. This summery tart deals with the glut in a very tasty way.

3–4 small courgettes
2 cloves garlic
150g cherry tomatoes
handful fresh basil leaves
1 x 125g ball fresh mozzarella cheese
4 large eggs
200ml cream
200ml milk
olive oil
salt and black pepper
1 pre-baked 28cm savoury tart case (see page 132)

Serves 4–6

Preheat the oven to 180°C (350°F), Gas Mark 4.

Wash the courgettes and cut into quarters lengthwise, then cut into 2cm pieces.

Peel and chop the garlic. Heat a frying pan and pour in enough olive oil to barely cover the bottom. Add the courgettes and cook them on a high heat for 3–4 minutes, tossing them frequently.

Add the garlic, season with a little salt and black pepper and cook for another couple of minutes. Don't let the garlic burn. Tip into the tart shell.

Wash the cherry tomatoes. Cut any large ones in half and place among the courgettes.

Tear the basil leaves and chop or tear the mozzarella into about 2cm pieces. Tuck both in among the courgettes and tomatoes.

Crack the eggs into a bowl, then whisk in the cream and milk. Season with 1 level tsp salt and ¼ tsp pepper. Pour the mix over the vegetables in the tart shell. Fill as much as you can without it coming over the edge. It's important the mix doesn't spill out as it will make the pastry soggy.

Bake for 20–25 minutes, until the filling is golden and set.

Kale, Gorgonzola and Pumpkin Tart

This is one of my favourite combos. It's a real autumn/winter tart when the pumpkins have been harvested and the kale is plentiful. It doesn't really matter which type of kale you use. We grow Cavalo de Nero, Red Russian and Asparagus kale and they are all tender enough to cook in a frying pan. If you have curly kale, blanch it in a pot of boiling water for a couple of minutes before proceeding with the recipe.

500g pumpkin or butternut squash
500g kale
½ tsp chilli flakes
1–2 cloves garlic, chopped
1 tsp fennel seeds
150g Gorgonzola, Crozier or Cashel Blue cheese
4 large eggs
200ml cream
200ml milk
olive oil
salt and black pepper
1 pre-baked 28cm tart case (see page 132)

Serves 4–6

Preheat the oven to 180°C (350°F), Gas Mark 4.

Peel the pumpkin and chop into 3cm pieces. Toss in a little olive oil with some salt and black pepper. Tip into a roasting tray and bake for 30 minutes, until the pumpkin is tender but not charred.

Wash the kale and strip out the tough stems by pulling the leaf up from the stem – it will come away easily. Chop the leaf into ribbons.

Heat a frying pan, add enough olive oil to just cover the bottom and add the chilli flakes, garlic and fennel seeds. Cook gently for a couple of minutes, taking care not to burn the garlic, then add the chopped kale. Stir everything together and cook over a medium heat for 4–5 minutes, until the kale has wilted and softened.

Put the cooled, roasted pumpkin pieces into the tart shell and tuck in the kale around it. Crumble the cheese on top.

Crack the eggs into a bowl, then whisk in the cream and milk. Season with 1 level tsp salt and ¼ tsp pepper. Pour the mix over the vegetables in the tart shell. Fill as much as you can without it coming over the edge. It's important the mix doesn't spill because it will make the pastry soggy.

Bake for 20–25 minutes, until the filling is golden and set.

Pissaladière Tart

This is our version of the Provençal favourite. Over time it has wandered away from the traditional combination of onion, anchovies and olives, but the anchovies can be used instead of the chèvre if that's your preference.

7 large onions
75ml olive oil
1 x 400g tin tomatoes
100g stoned black olives
150g goat's cheese – chèvre, St Tola or similar soft goat's cheese
salt and black pepper
1 pre-baked 28cm tart case (see page 132)

Serves 4–6

Peel the onions, cut in half and thinly slice. Heat a large frying pan and add the olive oil and the onions. Give them a good stir and season with a little salt. When you can hear the onions sizzling, turn the heat down. Cook slowly for about 1 hour, giving the occasional stir to prevent sticking until they are totally soft and golden. At this stage the onions should be sweet.

Preheat the oven to 180°C (350°F), Gas Mark 4.

Chop the tomatoes and stir into the onions together with the olives and cook on medium heat for a further 20 minutes, until the liquid from the tomatoes has reduced and the mixture is thick. Season with salt and pepper.

Tip the mixture into the tart shell and spread it out evenly. Cut the goat's cheese into thin pieces and place around the perimeter of the tart.

Bake for about 20 minutes or until the cheese looks toasty.

Roasted Beetroot, Rainbow Chard and Chèvre Tart

We grow lots of beetroot and rainbow chard in our walled garden and they make a great combination in a tart. If you can't find rainbow chard use regular chard; even spinach would make a good substitute. We roast the beetroot, which makes it quite sweet, but if you are in a hurry you could get away with boiling it.

5–6 small beetroots
500g rainbow chard
100g chèvre (creamy goat's cheese)
4 large eggs
200ml cream
200ml milk
olive oil
salt and black pepper
1 pre-baked 28cm tart case (see page 132)

Serves 4–6

Preheat the oven to 180°C (350°F), Gas Mark 4.

Wash the beetroots, place in a baking tray and rub with a little oil. Cover the baking tray with aluminium foil and roast in the oven for 60–90 minutes. Check to see if they are cooked by piercing with a sharp knife. If it slips in easily they are ready, if there is resistance, bake for a little longer. Allow to cool, then peel and chop into quarters.

Wash the chard. Remove the centre stems and chop them into 1cm pieces. Chop the leaves of the chard into 2cm ribbons. Heat a frying pan. Add enough olive oil to barely cover the bottom. Add the chopped stems and season with a little salt. Cook on a medium heat for 4–5 minutes, until the stems soften. Add the chard leaves to the pan. Cook for a couple more minutes, until the leaves wilt down. Taste – it may need a little more salt.

Put the beetroot, the chard stems and leaves into the tart shell. Crumble the chèvre on top.

Crack the eggs into a bowl and whisk in the cream and milk. Season with 1 level tsp salt and ¼ tsp pepper. Pour the mix over the vegetables in the tart shell. Fill as much as you can without it coming over the edge. It's important the mix doesn't spill because it will make the pastry soggy

Bake for 20–25 minutes, until the filling is golden and set.

Spinach, Sweet Potato and Comté Tart

Spinach tarts are always popular in our shop. Sometimes we make straightforward spinach and ricotta and other times this version with sweet potato. It's a little less eggy and more veggie than the other spinach tart and looks good with the bright yellow potato poking through.

1 large sweet potato (450g)
500g spinach
nutmeg
4 large eggs
200ml cream
200ml milk
100g Comté cheese, grated
olive oil
salt and black pepper
1 pre-baked 28cm tart case (see page 132)

Serves 4–6

Preheat the oven to 180°C (350°F), Gas Mark 4.

Peel the sweet potato, and cut into even-sized 3cm chunks. Toss in a little olive oil. Season with salt and pepper and put onto a roasting tray. Cook in the oven for 20 minutes, until tender.

Bring a large saucepan of water to the boil.

Wash the spinach and break off any big, tatty stems. Add some salt to the water, then the spinach. You may have to do this in two batches if you don't have a very big saucepan. As soon as the water comes back to the boil, remove the spinach and plunge into a large bowl of cold water. Drain and squeeze a little at a time to remove as much water as you can. Chop roughly, then give it another squeeze to get rid of any water that might have been trapped between the leaves. Season with a pinch of salt and grate a little nutmeg over – not too much. You want to be wondering what the extra flavour in the spinach is, not going aaah, nutmeg!

Crack the eggs into a bowl and whisk in the cream and milk. Season with 1 level tsp salt and ¼ tsp pepper.

Stir in the chopped spinach and grated cheese (Emmental or Gruyère are good too).

Put half of the sweet potatoes in the tart shell. Pour over the egg, spinach and cheese mix until the shell is three-quarters full. Arrange the remaining sweet potatoes around the top of the tart and fill any gaps with the remaining mix. It's important the mix doesn't spill or overflow because it will make the pastry soggy.

Bake for 20–25 minutes, until the filling is golden and set.

Savoury Pastry

This is the recipe for the savoury tart cases we make at our shop which we are always being asked for. It's made using the standard shortcrust pastry ratio of two parts flour to one part fat – butter is our choice. It's bound together with a little cold water so we have no big secrets. Success has more to do with the handling/non-handling of the pastry. Cold ingredients, a cool kitchen and a cold kitchen counter is ideal. You can mix it with your fingertips but if the day/kitchen is warm, run your hands under the cold tap halfway through. My nan reckoned she made better pastry by cutting through the butter with a fork so her fingers were kept out of contact with the fat altogether. In our recipe we use a food processor/mixer. We get the best results from using unbleached organic white flour but wholemeal works too. The most important thing is to avoid the pastry puffing up so check there are no raising agents in the flour. We use tart tins with a loose base so it's easy to remove the tart from the tin when it's baked. Ceramic dishes don't conduct heat well enough for good pastry.

300g unbleached white flour
150g chilled butter, cut into small dice
½ tsp salt
100–120ml ice-cold water

Makes 1 x 28cm tart case

Put the flour into the bowl of the food processor or mixer. Cut the chilled butter into small cubes and add to the bowl together with the salt. Pulse the mix in short blasts so the butter breaks into very small pieces in the flour. Don't be tempted to go too far. The butter has to be just incorporated and no more.

Add the water a little at a time and pulse briefly between additions until the pastry comes together. Again, don't overdo it. It's okay if there are a few bits that don't come together as you can incorporate them when you turn it out.

Tip the pastry and any odd bits onto a clean counter and quickly gather everything together with your hands. Do not knead it like bread dough. A couple of quick, light shoves with the heel of your hand should bring everything into one piece. Encourage the pastry into a round and flatten slightly, then wrap in a piece of parchment paper and chill for 1 hour.

Before rolling it's a good idea to briefly chill the counter; we use bags of frozen peas, which work very well. They won't defrost in this time.

Lightly dust the counter with some flour and put the pastry in the middle. Give it a couple of light rolls with a rolling pin, working away from you. Turn the pastry 45 degrees and roll again. Lift the pastry and sprinkle a little more flour onto the counter to prevent the pastry from sticking – not too much as you don't want to incorporate more flour into the pastry. Don't sprinkle flour on top of the pastry. If it's sticking to the rolling pin, flip the pastry over and put the sticky side down on the floured work surface.

Keep rolling, encouraging the pastry into a large circle until it's about as thick as a two euro coin, definitely not thinner, maybe marginally thicker. Make it bigger than the tart tin to allow for the sides. Feel with your fingertips around the edge of the pastry to check that it's evenly rolled.

Have the tart tin close to hand. Put the rolling pin onto the edge of the pastry closest to you, and carefully roll it away from you so that the pastry winds around the pin. Lift it up from the counter and slip the tart shell into the space in front of you. Unroll the pastry from the pin on top of the tart shell so that it covers the tart shell with a generous overhang. Don't let the rolling pin touch the edge of the tart shell or it will puncture it.

With your fingers, gently but firmly encourage the pastry into the side of the tin paying particular care that the edge around the base of the tin is filled. Straighten the upper edges with your fingers so that the pastry stands upright and trim with a sharp paring knife about 1 centimetre above the top edge of the tart shell. This is important as the pastry will shrink a little during cooking and if the sides shrink too much you won't fit in much filling.

Put the pastry shell into the fridge and chill for at least 2 hours. We usually chill ours overnight.

To bake, preheat the oven to 180°C (350°F), Gas Mark 4. Make sure the oven has reached this temperature before you put the pastry in, otherwise the pastry will melt.

We put the tart shells directly on the oven shelf without covering with paper or beans. It means we have to keep an eye on it for the first 5–10 minutes in case the sides collapse, but this way the pastry bakes evenly. If the sides collapse we take the shell out of the oven and gently push the sides back into position. If they keep falling down we prop them up with spoons. This isn't the norm, but it can happen.

If the bottom of the tart shell puffs up, wrap your hand in a tea towel and gently deflate the pastry. The hot steam will burn you if you don't protect yourself.

Bake the pastry shell until it is a good golden brown – about 15 minutes. The time will depend on the thickness of the pastry and the temperature of the oven. The important thing is to keep an eye on it, and if your oven has a hot spot and the tart bakes unevenly give it a turn to ensure it's evenly cooked. If the tart shell is undercooked you'll have a soggy bottom so be brave with the pre-baking. No blond tarts!

The tart shell is now ready to be filled.

While the tart shell can be used straight away, it will keep for at least 48 hours.

Crème Brûlée 136

Flan 138

Panna Cotta 140

Peaches Poached in White Wine 142

Rhubarb Clafoutis 144

Strawberry and Mascarpone Tart 146

Blackberry Crumble 148

French Apple Tart 150

Lime and Coconut Tart 152

Christmas Clementines 154

Pumpkin and Coconut Cake 156

Tarte au Chocolat 158

Chocolate and Hazelnut Cake 160

Summer Fruit Jam 162

Sweet Pastry 164

Peach Bellini 166

Sweet

Things

Crème Brûlée

If you come to our house for lunch or dinner it is quite likely you will be served Flan, Crème Brûlée or Panna Cotta. All three are milky or creamy desserts which are very quick to put together. Crème Brûlée sounds quite fancy, but it just means burnt cream. It can be a little bit daunting to make but is no bother if you use our fail-safe method. The classic version is a set custard with a caramelised top but we like putting fruit under the custard. It makes it a lighter and fresher dessert without taking away from the moreish custard. You can use whatever fruit is in season – rhubarb, plums, blackcurrants or gooseberries – whatever you fancy or have to hand.

300g fruit of your choice poached with a little sugar until soft
125g caster sugar
5 large egg yolks
1 tsp plain white flour or pinch cornflour
400ml cream
½ vanilla pod, split lengthwise

Serves 6

Put a big tablespoon of fruit into each of six ramekins or teacups and set aside.

Put 75g of the sugar, egg yolks and flour into a bowl (the flour prevents the eggs from scrambling when heated later; this is what usually goes wrong and puts people off making this dish). Using cornflower makes it gluten-free. Whisk for a few minutes to thick ribbons, when the whisk, when lifted from the mix, leaves a trail. At this stage the sugar will have dissolved into the eggs and air will have lightened the mixture.

Pour the cream into a saucepan. Scrape the inside of the vanilla pod into the cream and pop the pod in as well. Slowly bring to the boil.

Beat the heated cream into the egg mix, then return it all to the saucepan and heat gently over a medium heat. Keep heating and stirring until the mix is thick enough to coat the back of a spoon. Don't allow it to come to the boil, as it could scramble. Remove the vanilla pod.

Pour over the fruit in the ramekins and chill. At this stage they can be kept in the fridge for a couple of days.

Before serving, generously sprinkle a light coating of the remaining caster sugar over the top of each pot and caramelise with a blow torch or under the grill.

Flan

I think of *flan* as the national dessert of Spain as it's on just about every menu, sometimes homemade, sometimes arriving in a little plastic pot. In France it's called crème caramel. Our kids loved it when they were small and they weren't that particular as to whether it was homemade or shop bought. It's one of those simple desserts you're almost guaranteed to be able to make with what you have in the house. It's fast to make and impressive when turned out. They are usually baked in little metal moulds, but teacups do a good job too.

4 heaped tbsp granulated sugar
2 tbsp water

600ml full fat milk
3 large eggs + 2 yolks
2 tbsp sugar or honey
1 tsp vanilla essence

Serves 6

Put the sugar and water into a small pot and heat slowly until the sugar melts. Increase the heat to moderate and cook until the sugar caramelises. As soon as the sugar turns a deep golden colour, remove from the heat as it will continue cooking with the heat of the pan. Carefully pour into 6 moulds, covering the base only.

Preheat the oven to 180°C (350°F), Gas Mark 4.

Put the milk, eggs, 2 tbsp sugar or honey and vanilla into a bowl and mix together gently until smooth (don't overbeat). Gently ladle into the moulds.

Place the moulds in a deep roasting dish and pour boiling water around them to come halfway up the sides.

Carefully place in the oven and bake for 20–25 minutes, until the custard is just set. Allow to cool.

To serve, run a knife around the edge of each mould and turn out onto a plate.

Panna Cotta

I always have room after dinner to squeeze in a panna cotta. This wonderful, wibbly Italian dessert just slips down beautifully. It can be made with various combinations of milk, cream or buttermilk; these are all interchangeable. It's set with gelatine so is unsuitable for vegetarians. I have tried to make it with carrageen moss but the result was more bounce than wibble. I think I need to try again sometime, maybe with agar agar. Meanwhile, I am happy with this version.

5 sheets gelatine
400ml milk
500ml cream
200g sugar
1 vanilla pod

Serves 6

Put the gelatine sheets into cold water to soften.

Line 6 moulds or cups with clingfilm.

Put the milk and cream into a saucepan with the sugar. Split the vanilla pod, scrape the seeds into the milk and add the vanilla pod. Bring to the boil and take off the heat.

Take the gelatine sheets out of the cold water, shake off any excess water and stir into the milk mixture. Allow to cool slightly before removing the vanilla pod and pouring into the moulds.

Cool and chill until serving.

To serve, upend the moulds onto plates and gently peel away the clingfilm. Add a couple of spoonfuls of poached or fresh fruit around the outside.

Peaches Poached in White Wine

This is an almost pain-free dessert if you can bear to part with some white wine. If it is elderflower season add a few sprigs of elderflowers to the syrup, otherwise a good splash of elderflower cordial will also do the trick. Whichever method you use it will give a delicious twist to this simple dish. Ideal for a summer party, it can be cooked a day or two in advance.

500g sugar
250ml water
250ml white wine
2 sprigs elderflowers or 1 tbsp elderflower cordial
6 peaches

Serves 6

Put the sugar, water and wine in a saucepan and bring to the boil. When it clears, add the elderflowers or cordial and set aside.

Cut the peaches in half and put into the elderflower syrup and return to the heat to gently poach for 5–10 minutes. The cooking time depends on the size and ripeness of the peaches. When cooked, the peaches will still be firm but the skins should peel off.

You can reduce the poaching syrup by boiling it rapidly and serve it with the peaches or use it on its own with ice cream later.

Serve with the best vanilla ice cream you can find.

Rhubarb Clafoutis

When the new season rhubarb is available this is an impressively simple dessert to make. A variation on the French classic, to be a true clafoutis it would need to be baked with cherries but if we stuck to that we wouldn't get to eat many clafoutis as in Ireland cherries are pretty scarce. This is a batter-based custard baked in the oven. Easy peasy. No pastry or anything complicated, just whisk the ingredients together and pour over roasted or poached fruit and pop in the oven. It makes a great dessert and if you take the time to arrange the fruit on top it looks quite elegant.
The clafoutis can be baked in any ovenproof dish or baking tin, ideally 20–24cm in diameter. For individual portions use buttered ramekins.

6 stalks rhubarb
170g caster sugar
4 large eggs
50g white flour (or polenta if you want gluten-free)
50g ground almonds
250ml cream
1 tsp vanilla extract
15g butter to grease dish

Serves 4–6

Preheat the oven to 180°C (350°F), Gas Mark 4.

Wash the rhubarb and cut into 5cm lengths. Toss in about 20g of the sugar and put onto a baking tray. Bake in the oven for 12 minutes. The rhubarb should be sweating at this stage with the juices beginning to run.

Crack the eggs into a bowl then add the remaining sugar, flour and ground almonds. Whisk to a smooth paste.

Put the cream into a small saucepan with the vanilla and bring to the boil.

Whisk the cream into the egg mix.

Rub a baking dish with butter and pour in two-thirds of the mix. Arrange the rhubarb on top and drizzle over the remaining batter.

Bake in the oven for 35–40 minutes. Check after 30 minutes just in case your oven is particularly hot. The clafoutis is cooked when it is set and golden all over.

Serve at room temperature with whipped cream on the side.

Strawberry and Mascarpone Tart

I'm all for quick tricks when it comes to making dessert. This recipe not only uses quick tricks, like whisking mascarpone and cream together for the filling, but it's also possible to cheat by buying a pastry or flan case to put the filling into. Of course the result will only be as good as the ingredients, so if you have the time to make and bake a sweet tart shell all the better. Our recipe is well worth the trouble. Strawberries are an obvious choice for the topping but all the summer fruits – blackcurrants, gooseberries, peaches and apricots – work very well. Using jam sugar is an excellent trick for glazing sweet tarts: just cook the sugar in water and it's guaranteed to set. The tart will look super professional!

250g mascarpone
250ml cream
50g sugar
1 tsp rose water
500g strawberries
2 tbsp jam sugar
1 tbsp water
1 pre-baked 28cm sweet tart case (see page 164)

Serves 4–6

Put the mascarpone and cream into a bowl with the sugar and gently mix together, then whisk until stiff. Stir in the rose water.

Tip the mascarpone cream into the tart shell and spread it out evenly.

Halve or quarter the strawberries, depending on how big they are, and arrange them on top.

Put the jam sugar and water into a small saucepan and gently melt. Boil for a couple of minutes, then brush over the fruit to glaze.

Blackberry Crumble

This is a real classic which is not often made in these days of shop-bought tarts and cakes. It is difficult to beat with its buttery, crunchy crumb over fruit that's melted down and oozing with juicy blackberryness. Also known as 'nana's crumble' in our house, we all phone my mum to ask her for this recipe as, while very simple to make, we always forget the recipe in between the blackberry seasons. My mum finds this pretty strange as we're meant to be able to cook! The fruit can of course be changed to suit the seasons – rhubarb, gooseberries, all sorts of summer fruits, but blackberries always inspire us to make this.

4 cooking apples
100g caster sugar
lemon juice
500g blackberries
75g butter
75g demerara sugar
175g flour

Serves 4–6

Peel and core the apples and chop into small pieces. Put into a saucepan, sprinkle with caster sugar and squeeze a little lemon juice on top. Give the pot a shake to mix everything together. Put on a gentle heat and cover with a lid. Give the pot a shake every few minutes and cook until the apples have begun to melt down. Take off the heat and cool completely.

Put the apples into a medium-sized ovenproof dish and scatter the raw blackberries on top.

Preheat the oven to 180°C (350°F), Gas Mark 4.

Rub the butter into the demerara sugar and flour with the fingertips, until it is like breadcrumbs.

Sprinkle the crumble mix over everything and bake for about 20 minutes, until golden brown. Delicious every time!

French Apple Tart

This impressive looking tart sits in the quick tricks department. Shop-bought puff pastry works well but buy the best you can find. Butter puff pastry tastes best so check the ingredients when buying – if you have a choice – and opt for the one with the highest butter content.

2–3 cooking apples
50g granulated sugar
¼ tsp ground cinnamon
25g butter (optional)
2–3 eating apples
juice ½ lemon
500g puff pastry
1 egg
2 tbsp milk
2 tbsp sure-set jam sugar

Serves 4–6

Peel and chop the cooking apples and put into a small saucepan with the sugar, cinnamon and butter, if using (it will make a richer purée). If you aren't using butter, add a couple of drops of water. Put the pan on a medium heat and cover with a lid. Give the pot a shake every few minutes and when the apples start to cook, turn the heat down and leave until they have reduced to a mush. Beat with a wooden spoon until smooth. Leave to cool completely, otherwise they will melt the pastry.

Preheat the oven to 180°C (350°F), Gas Mark 4.

Peel and core the eating apples. Cut into thin slices and toss in the lemon juice.

Roll out the puff pastry, keeping it in a neat rectangle as far as possible. (It is also possible to buy the pastry already rolled in sheets, in which case just carefully unroll). Place on a baking tray. Using a small, sharp knife, score a border about 1cm wide all the way around the pastry, taking care not to cut through. This will rise without the weight of the fruit and form a border, keeping in the apple slices.

Beat the egg and milk with a fork and brush lightly on the outer border – be careful not to flood the scored line.

Spoon the cooled apple purée on the inner rectangle and arrange the sweet apple slices, overlapping, on top. The apple slices will shrink a little when cooked so don't space them too far apart.

Bake for about 20 minutes until golden.

Put the sure-set sugar in a small saucepan with enough water to just melt it, and cook on a high heat for a few minutes. Carefully brush over the cooked tart. This is a quick trick to glaze the tart and give it a professional finish – it sure beats boiling and straining jam and sugar.

Lime and Coconut Tart

This is a tart with a tropical edge. Just the mention of lime and coconuts brings to mind sunshine and palm trees.

200g caster sugar
3 large eggs
3 limes, zest and juice
375ml cream
200g desiccated coconut
1 pre-baked 28cm sweet pastry case (see page 164)

Serves 4–6

Preheat the oven to 180°C (350°F), Gas Mark 4.

Whisk together the sugar, eggs, lime zest and juice until evenly blended.

Stir in the cream and coconut.

Pour the mix into the tart case and bake for approx. 20–25 minutes until golden and wibbly (the tart will firm up as it cools).

Christmas Clementines

These juicy, sweet, fragrant fruits make an excellent dessert when served with some good quality vanilla ice cream. It's an easy, fresh option to offer as an alternative to Christmas pudding. The only crucial implement for this recipe is a sharp knife.

10–12 clementines/tangerines
225g granulated sugar
225ml warm water
5cm cinnamon stick
30ml Cointreau/Grand Marnier

Serves 4–6

Peel the rind from two of the clementines and cut it into fine strips.

Peel the remainder, removing all traces of pith from the fruit, and put into a bowl.

Put the sugar into a small saucepan and add a couple of tablespoons of cold water to dissolve the sugar. Heat gently until the sugar melts, then increase the heat and cook the sugar until it caramelises and turns a rich, nutty brown. Remove from the heat. Wrap a tea towel around your hand to protect it and slowly pour in the warm water.

Add the peel and cinnamon stick to the syrup, return to the heat and cook for 5 minutes. Remove from the heat and leave to cool.

Add the Cointreau/Grand Marnier to the syrup and pour over the fruit. Cover and chill for a few hours or, better still, overnight.

Pumpkin and Coconut Cake

I love cakes that use vegetables. They are always moist and sound fairly healthy, in spite of all the sugar. I use light muscovado sugar which has great flavour but don't be put off if you don't have that in the house, just use whatever you have, it will still work. The pumpkin is of the bright orange/deep yellow dense flesh variety, Crown Prince or Queensland Blue are my favourites, but a butternut squash will do if that's all you can find. A Halloween pumpkin won't do the job.

200g finely ground wholemeal flour
1 tsp cinnamon
¼ tsp ground cardamom
1 heaped tsp baking powder
100g desiccated coconut
225g butter
300g brown sugar
3 large eggs
200g peeled and grated pumpkin

Icing
150g coconut oil
zest 1 well-scrubbed lemon
150g icing sugar
20g shaved coconut*

* Coconut shavings are available in many health and wholefood shops.

Serves 6–8

Preheat the oven to 180°C (350°F), Gas Mark 4.

Prepare a 24cm loose-bottomed cake tin. Oil or butter the base and sides of the tin. Cut a circle of parchment or greaseproof paper and fit it at the base.

Measure out all the dry ingredients – flour, spices, baking powder and coconut – and set aside.

Put the butter and sugar into a food processor or mixing bowl and cream together until the mix loosens and is smooth.

Add the eggs, one by one, with the machine running if you're using a food processor, mixing to incorporate well. If it looks like it's going to split add a spoonful of the flour combo.

Add all the dry ingredients to the wet mix and when well combined add the pumpkin and mix briefly.

Pour into the prepared tin and bake for about 45 minutes, until a knife inserted comes out clean and the sides of the cake shrink from the tin.

Leave the cake to cool completely before taking it out of the tin.

For the icing, beat the coconut oil, lemon zest and icing sugar together in a bowl – don't use a food processor because it will become too runny. Spread on top of cake. Toast the shaved coconut in the oven for a few minutes – it will brown very quickly. They can be toasted when the cake comes out of the oven to save re-heating it. Scatter the coconut over the top of the cake and leave to set for 30 minutes before serving.

Tarte au Chocolat

Once you have a pre-baked sweet tart shell this recipe is simplicity itself. There really isn't anything to it other than finding good quality chocolate. You're pretty much guaranteed to receive compliments!

500g chocolate (55–70% cocoa solids)
3 large eggs
150ml milk
350ml cream
chocolate curls or a few strawberries to garnish
1 pre-cooked 28cm sweet pastry case (see page 164)

Serves 6–8

Preheat the oven to 180°C (350°F), Gas Mark 4.

Melt the chocolate in a bowl set over a saucepan of boiling water.

Meanwhile whisk the eggs in a bowl.

Put the milk and cream into a saucepan and heat until boiling. Whisk onto the eggs, then whisk in the melted chocolate.

Pour the mix into the pre-baked tart shell and place in the oven*. Turn the oven off and leave the tart in the oven until it has cooled – about an hour. Chill before serving.

Decorate the tart with chocolate curls or strawberries to serve.

*If there is any leftover mix pour it into a cup or ramekin and pop it into the oven with the tart. You'll have a bonus mini pot au chocolat.

Chocolate and Hazelnut Cake

This has to be one of the yummiest chocolate cakes ever. We have been baking it for the past ten years and we still enjoy eating it; this is quite something as after a few hundred of anything we seem to lose interest, but the chocolate cake has passed the test of time. It is made with hazelnuts instead of flour, which makes it gluten-free and also gives it a long life. If you can resist eating this in one go – it is a pretty big cake – you will find it keeps perfectly for days if you wrap it up or put it into a cake tin. There's a very social aspect to making this cake known as the 'hot rub'. After roasting the hazelnuts, wrap them in a tea towel and rub them on somebody's back and shoulders. Delicious. If you can't find a friend, just rub yourself. This will loosen the skins so you can pick the nuts out. Do not leave the hazelnuts lying around wrapped in the tea towel as chances are you, or someone else, will take it to do something else and the hazelnuts will escape all over the kitchen!

150g hazelnuts
300g chocolate (minimum 55% cocoa solids)
150g caster sugar + 1 tbsp
150g butter, cut into small pieces
6 large eggs, separated

Topping
100g butter
150g chocolate

Serves 6–8

Preheat the oven to 180°C (350°F), Gas Mark 4.

Put the hazelnuts on a tray and roast for about 10 minutes, until the skins loosen. Wrap in a towel and rub the hazelnuts to remove the skins. Sort the nuts from the skins, then put the skinned hazelnuts into the food processor and grind until fairly fine. Tip them into a bowl and set aside.

Reduce the temperature of the oven to 160°C (325°F), Gas Mark 3.

Grease a 24cm springform cake tin.

Sit a bowl on top of a saucepan of simmering water, making sure the base of the bowl doesn't touch the water. Add the chocolate to the bowl and heat gently until it melts.

Put the 150g of sugar and butter into a food processor and process until smooth and light in colour. You'll have to scrape down the sides with a spatula a couple of times.

With the processor on add the egg yolks followed by the melted chocolate and finally the ground hazelnuts.

As soon as everything is mixed together tip into a mixing bowl.

Whisk the egg whites to soft peaks, add a tablespoon of the sugar and continue whisking to stiff peaks. If using a mixer be sure to stop as soon as stiff peaks are reached or the egg whites will become dry and difficult to fold into the mix.

Fold the egg whites into the chocolate mix.

Tip the mix into the tin and gently smooth over – don't muck about too much, otherwise the air you've folded in will escape.

Bake for about 40 minutes until a sharp knife inserted into the centre of the cake comes out clean.

To make the topping, put the chocolate and butter into a small bowl and sit it over a saucepan of simmering water, without letting the water touch the bottom of the bowl. When the chocolate and butter have melted, mix them together. Allow to cool and thicken enough to spread over the cake.

Decorate the cake with chocolate curls or a little grated chocolate.

Summer Fruit Jam

We have plenty of fruit bushes in our garden – gooseberries, blackcurrants and redcurrants. They are all ripe and ready for picking in July, just when we're mad busy and the to-do list is on overload, so the fruit gets picked and whatever we can't use immediately in summer fruit tarts, we freeze for jam-making later. This is actually quite a bonus when it comes to jam-making as freezing fruit makes it expand and the cell walls collapse. This is why frozen fruit always collapses when defrosted. When we defrost the fruit to make jam the pectin in the hundreds of little pips is ready to run. Pectin is a jam-maker's friend. It makes the jam set so if it's ready to go the jam can be made quickly. It will also look brighter and more beautiful because it will reach setting-point faster. Some fruits are higher in pectin than others. Strawberries and raspberries, for instance, can use the help of a little lemon juice, but my combo is usually blackcurrants, gooseberries and redcurrants, which don't need any help at all.

500g gooseberries
500g blackcurrants
500g redcurrants
1.5 kg granulated sugar
8–10 clean jam jars with lids

Put the fruit into the saucepan and pour over the sugar. With the heat on low, gently allow the fruit to melt, then stir in the sugar until dissolved.

Increase the heat and bring to the boil. Keep the jam at a rolling boil. You don't need to stir it anymore, it'll do this for itself, but don't wander off because you need to keep an eye on the pot. If it looks like the jam is going to boil over, decrease the heat slightly. Cook at a rapid boil for about 15 minutes.

Put a small plate into the freezer to chill.

Wash the jam jars. Pop them into a preheated oven, 180°C (350°F), Gas Mark 4, for 5 minutes to sterilise them.

When the 15 minutes of boiling is up, put about half a teaspoon of jam on the cold plate and leave it to cool – you can keep the jam cooking while you do this. When the jam has cooled give the surface a little shove and if it gently wrinkles, it's ready. If it isn't ready, continue boiling rapidly for another 5 minutes and try again.

Pour the jam into the hot jars (if you put it into cold jars they will crack), give them a wipe to remove any spills and cover immediately with clean lids.

Jam is best made in small batches – I don't like making more than 3 kg at any one time even though I have a very large pot. It's probably best to try 500g of each in your biggest saucepan and see how you go. Jam needs to be boiled rapidly to achieve a set and if there's too much in the pot it's difficult to get it to stay in the pot. Cleaning up boiled-over jam is no joke!

Sweet Pastry

Our sweet pastry recipe takes a little patience and pre-planning as it's impossible to roll out when it's first made. It needs at least three hours in the fridge to firm up and ideally should be left overnight. We use unsalted butter. Irish butter is quite salty and we don't want the taste of salt in our sweet tarts. It can be made using a food processor or a mixer using the pastry blade. Both methods are explained in the recipe. The recipe may initially seem back to front, but if you follow the instructions your pastry will be crisp, melt in the mouth and you will receive plenty of compliments. It's best to make enough for a couple of tarts while you're at it and freeze half for the next baking session.

125g unsalted butter
100g icing sugar
1 large egg
250g plain white flour, ideally unbleached

Makes 1 x 28cm sweet pastry case

Mixer method
Chop the butter into 2cm pieces and place in the mixer bowl with the sugar. Turn on the mixer and slowly increase the speed until the butter and sugar come together. Continue mixing until they become soft and creamy.

Add the egg and mix until the mixture is even and creamy again.

Turn the machine off and add half the flour. Mix at a medium speed until the flour is incorporated. Don't go at full speed or you will end up in a cloud of flour. Add the remaining flour and mix again until the pastry barely comes together. Stop as soon as this happens. Don't overmix otherwise the pastry will become chewy.

Food processor method
Chop the butter into 2cm pieces and place in the processor with the sugar. Pulse a few times or until the butter breaks down a little. Turn the machine on full, and when the butter and sugar are blended together add the egg through the chute in the lid. Pulse until the mixture is smooth and creamy again.

Turn the machine off, take off the lid and add half the flour. Process until the flour and butter are incorporated and repeat with the remaining flour. Stop as soon as the mixture is barely together. Do not over process.

Next ...
Spread a large piece of parchment paper on the counter and dump the mixture out of the bowl into the centre. Pick up the sides of the paper and encourage the pastry into a mass. Roll the pastry up in the paper and put into the fridge to chill for a minimum of 3 hours, but better still overnight.

Everything must be cool when you're rolling pastry so working in a hot kitchen or in the summer can be a nightmare. A good trick is to use a packet of frozen peas or something similar to chill the counter for a few minutes before you start.

To roll the pastry, dust a clean surface with a little flour. Compress a piece of pastry, keeping the round shape. Lift the pastry, sprinkle a light dusting of flour on the surface once more and turn the pastry over. Using a rolling pin, roll the pastry away from you a couple of times then turn the pastry 90 degrees and repeat. Continue rolling and turning until the pastry is 3–4 mm thick.

Hold the rolling pin just above and at the front of the pastry and carefully roll the pastry onto the rolling pin. Slip the tart shell underneath and unroll the pastry on top of it. Tuck the pastry into the shell taking care not to stretch it, otherwise it will shrink when it cooks. Press the pastry into the sides of the tin then knock the excess off the top with the heel of your hand. Run your fingers around the sides once again, pressing the pastry and straightening up the sides. This should make the pastry rise very slightly above the edge of the tin.

Chill for at least 1 hour, longer is better. If you are really short of time chill the pastry in the deep freeze for 15–20 minutes.

Preheat the oven to 180°C (350°F), Gas Mark 4.

Bake the tart for 10–15 minutes. You can put in pastry beans or silver foil but I find it prevents the pastry from browning. I just keep an eye on it and check that the sides of the tart don't collapse. If the base of the tart puffs up, wrap your hand in a tea towel and gently deflate it, being careful of the hot steam.

When the pastry is lightly golden take it out of the oven. It's then ready to fill.

This recipe can easily be doubled and the pastry frozen. The rolled-out case can also be kept chilled in the fridge for a few days.

Peach Bellini

We have a peach tree in our polytunnel, espaliered against the wall. Each spring the tree is covered in beautiful pink blossoms which we tickle with a feather to aid pollination just in case enough bees don't find their way in to do the job. This guarantees hundreds of peaches. It's an incredible sight every July as peach trees are few and far between in West Cork. They all ripen within a two-week period so there is quite some eating to do. The first peaches are simply eaten ripe off the tree, but as the end of the first week finishes they start creeping into the sweet tarts we make in the shop. The windfalls are used to make peach chutney and then there is the Bellini party. Bellinis are a fun thing to make with peaches and also provide a good excuse to invite a few friends around. These alcoholic smoothies are best enjoyed in the sunshine.

3–4 ripe peaches
1 tbsp grenadine (optional)
150ml peach schnapps
1 bottle chilled Prosecco
ice cubes

Fills 8-10 Champagne flutes

Stone the peaches and liquidise until smooth.
Strain through a sieve.

Add the grenadine and schnapps and chill.
If you are in rush, add some ice cubes immediately.

To serve, fill about one third of the glass with the peach purée and top up with chilled Prosecco.
Give it a good stir and drink immediately.

Gluten-free recipes

Salads
Asian Slaw 12
Beetroot, Caramelised Goat's Cheese and Pumpkin Seed Salad 14
Carrot, Avocado and Wakame Salad 16
Green Bean Salad with Lemon and Parmesan 19
Jen's Broccoli Salad 20
Red Cabbage, Celeriac, Apple and Hazelnut Salad 22
Raul's Catalan Artichokes with Aioli 24
Quinoa and Chickpea Salad 28
Puy Lentil, Pea, Feta and Mint Salad 31
Summer Chickpea and Tuna Salad 32
New Potato and Smoked Mackerel Salad 34
Som Tam 36

Soups
Spring Minestrone Soup 42
Spinach Soup GF alternative 44
Rooty Toot Soup 51
Thai Pumpkin Soup 49

Fishy Dishes
Fish en Papillote 54
Thai Sweet and Sour Mackerel 56
Fish in Pakora Batter with Spicy Wedges 58
Grilled Cod with Roasted Cherry Tomatoes and Basil 61
Grilled Prawns with Whiskey Mayonnaise 63
Moroccan Fish Tagine 64
Red Curry over Fish 66
Fish Stock 72

Chorizo Infiltration
Chorizo and Bean Soup with Kale 76
Chickpeas and Chorizo 80
Chorizo and Cabbage Paella 82

Vegetarian Mains
Falafel Burgers with Tahini and Lemon Sauce 94
Lentil and Sweet Potato Burgers with Yellow Pepper Sauce 96
Borlotti Bean and Vegetable Stew 98
Summer Vegetable Pilaf with Yoghurt Sauce 100
Cassoulet of Summer Vegetables 102
Courgette and Herb Bake 104
Pindi Channa 106
Poor Man's Potatoes 110
Spicy Lentils with Grilled Halloumi Cheese 112
Thai Yellow Curry with Peanut Salsa 114
Vegetarian Moussaka 116
Rocket and Pumpkin Seed Pesto 118

Sweet Things
Crème Brûlée GF alternative 136
Flan 138
Panna Cotta 140
Peaches Poached in White Wine 142
Christmas Clementines 154
Chocolate and Hazelnut Cake 160
Summer Fruit Jam 162
Peach Bellini 166

We opened our shop in Clonakilty, *The Lettercollum Kitchen Project*, built a kitchen at the back and began to make food using all our beautiful produce.
It was good to have a day job and it also gave us the opportunity to travel again. We did miss the creativity of putting food on plates, but this was remedied by our taking groups of Irish people to Spain and France to teach them how to cook.

thanks ...

I would like to thank our family – Ronan, Hazel, Darragh, Raul, cousin Lenny and little Fionn for telling me I could do this and for being such willing guinea pigs.

Bridget Healy, Danni Dickson-McLellan, Flavie Chimines, Joe Capener, Sandra Plescher, Stu, Dom and Suzy for all their hard work and good humour in the shop.

Lorena Basso, the number one woofer who kept the garden together while I was totally distracted with this book.

Roz Crowley for organising me and egging me on.

Arna Rún Rúnarsdóttir for her photographs and Jean-Marcel Coulombeau for his photographs.

Etain Hickey of Etain Hickey Collections in Clonakilty, Mary Lincoln of Ardmore Pottery in Waterford.

June, Eric, Sandra and Chris; all of whom generously loaned their plates, bowls and contents of their kitchens for the photo shoot.

And most of all I would like to thank my husband and partner Con McLoughlin, for all his support and for bringing me here in the first place!

KAREN AUSTIN

Index

Aioli with Raul's Catalan Artichokes 24
Apple, French Tart 150
Apple, Red Cabbage, Celeriac and Hazelnut Salad 22
Artichokes with Aioli, Raul's Catalan 24
Asian Slaw 12
Aubergines in Vegetarian Moussaka 116
Avocado, Carrot and Wakame Salad 16

Bake, Courgette and Herb 104
Basil with Grilled Cod with Roasted Cherry Tomatoes 61
Basil, Courgette, Tomato and Mozzarella Tart 122
Batter, Pakora, Fish with Spicy Wedges 58
Bean and Chorizo Soup with Kale 76
Bean, Borlotti and Vegetable Stew 98
Beetroot, Caramelised Goat's Cheese and Pumpkin Seed Salad 14
Beetroot, Roasted, Rainbow Chard and Chèvre Tart 128
Bellini, Peach 166
Blackberry Crumble 148
Borlotti Bean and Vegetable Stew 98
Broccoli Salad, Jen's 20
Brûlée, Crème 136
Burgers, Falafel, with Tahini and Lemon Sauce 94
Burgers, Lentil and Sweet Potato with Yellow Pepper Sauce 96
Butterbean and Leek Gratin 108

Cabbage and Chorizo Paella 82
Cabbage in Asian Slaw 12
Cake, Chocolate and Hazelnut 160
Cake, Pumpkin and Coconut 156
Carrot, Avocado and Wakame Salad 16
Cassoulet of Summer Vegetables 102
Catalan Fish Stew 71
Celeriac, Red Cabbage, Apple and Hazelnut Salad 22
Chard, Rainbow, Roasted Beetroot and Chèvre Tart 128
Cheese, Grilled Halloumi with Spicy Lentils 112
Chèvre, Roasted Beetroot and Rainbow Chard Tart 128
Chickpea and Quinoa Salad 28
Chickpea and Tuna Summer Salad 32
Chickpeas and Chorizo 80
Chickpeas, in Pindi Channa 106
Chocolat, Tarte au 158
Chocolate and Hazelnut Cake 160
Chorizo and Bean Soup with Kale 76
Chorizo and Cabbage Paella 82
Chorizo and Chickpeas 80
Chorizo and Potato Tart 78
Chowder, Seafood 68
Christmas Clementines 154
Clafoutis, Rhubarb 144
Clementines, Christmas 154

Coconut and Lime Tart 153
Coconut and Pumpkin Cake 156
Cod, Grilled with Roasted Cherry Tomatoes and Basil 61
Comté, Spinach and Sweet Potato Tart 130
Courgette and Herb Bake 104
Courgette, Tomato, Basil and Mozzarella Tart 122
Crème Brûlée 136
Crème Caramel 138
Crumble, Blackberry 148
Curry, Red over Fish 66
Curry, Thai Yellow with Peanut Salsa 114

En Papillote, Fish 54

Falafel Burgers with Tahini and Lemon Sauce 94
Feta, Puy Lentil, Pea and Mint Salad 30
Filo and Pumpkin Parcels with Sweet Red Pepper Sauce 86
Fish en Papillote 54
Fish in Pakora Batter with Spicy Wedges 58
Fish Stew, Catalan 71
Fish Stock 72
Fish, Moroccan Tagine 64
Fish, Red Curry Over 66
Flan 138
French Apple Tart 150
Fruit, Summer Jam 162

Gazpacho 41
Gnocchi, Spinach and Ricotta with Tomato Sauce 92
Goat's Cheese, Beetroot and Pumpkin Seed Salad 14
Gorgonzola, Kale and Pumpkin Tart 124
Gratin, Leek and Butterbean 108
Green Bean Salad with Lemon and Parmesan 19
Grilled Cod with Roasted Cherry Tomatoes and Basil 61
Grilled Prawns with Whiskey Mayonnaise 63

Halloumi Cheese, Grilled with Spicy Lentils 112
Hazelnut and Chocolate Cake 160
Herb and Courgette Bake 104

Jam, Summer Fruit 162
Jen's Broccoli Salad 20

Kale, Chorizo and Bean Soup 76
Kale, Gorgonzola and Pumpkin Tart 124

Leek and Butterbean Gratin 108
Leek, Sweet Potato and Spelt Soup 46
Lemon and Parmesan in Green Bean Salad 19
Lemon and Tahini Sauce with Falafel Burgers 94
Lentil and Sweet Potato Burgers with Yellow Pepper Sauce 96
Lentil, Puy, Pea and Mint Salad 31
Lentils, Spicy with Grilled Halloumi Cheese 112
Lime and Coconut Tart 153
Linguine with Tomato and Mozzarella 90

Mackerel, Thai Sweet and Sour 56
Mascarpone and Strawberry Tart 146
Mayonnaise, Whiskey with Grilled Prawns 63
Minestrone, Spring Soup 42
Mint, Puy Lentil, Pea, Salad 31
Moroccan Fish Tagine 64
Moussaka, Vegetarian 116
Mozzarella with Linguine and Tomato 90
Mozzarella, Courgette, Tomato and Basil Tart 122

Nectarine, Pink Peppercorn and Mint Tabbouleh 27
New Potato and Smoked Mackerel Salad 34

Paella, Chorizo and Cabbage 82
Pakora Batter, Fish with Spicy Wedges 58
Panna Cotta 140
Parcels, Pumpkin and Filo with Sweet Red Pepper Sauce 86
Parmesan, in Green Bean and Lemon Salad 19
Pasta Primavera 88
Pastry, Savoury 132
Pastry, Sweet 164
Patatas a lo Pobre 110
Pea, Puy Lentil and Mint Salad 31
Peach Bellini 166
Peaches Poached in White Wine 142
Peanut Salsa with Thai Yellow Curry 114
Pepper Sauce, Yellow with Lentil and Sweet Potato Burgers 96
Pesto, Rocket and Pumpkin Seed 118
Pilaf, Summer Vegetable with Yoghurt Sauce 100
Pindi Channa 106
Pink Peppercorn, Nectarine and Mint Tabbouleh 27
Pissaladière Tart 126
Poor Man's Potatoes 110
Potato and Chorizo Tart 78
Potato, New and Smoked Mackerel Salad 34
Potatoes, Poor Man's 110
Prawns, Grilled with Whiskey Mayonnaise 63
Primavera, Pasta 88
Pumpkin and Coconut Cake 156
Pumpkin and Filo Parcels with Sweet Red Pepper Sauce 86
Pumpkin Seed and Rocket Pesto 118
Pumpkin Seed, Goat's Cheese, Beetroot Salad 14
Pumpkin, Kale and Gorgonzola Tart 124
Pumpkin. Thai Soup 49
Puy Lentil, Pea, Feta and Mint Salad 31

Quinoa and Chickpea Salad 28

Rainbow Chard, Chèvre and Roasted Beetroot Tart 128
Raul's Catalan Artichokes with Aioli 24
Red Cabbage, Celeriac, Apple and Hazelnut Salad 22
Red Curry Over Fish 66
Red Pepper Sauce with Pumpkin and Filo

Parcels 86
Rhubarb Clafoutis 144
Ricotta, Gnocchi and Spinach with Tomato Sauce 92
Roasted Beetroot, Rainbow Chard and Chèvre Tart 128
Roasted Cherry Tomatoes and Basil, with Grilled Cod 61
Rocket and Pumpkin Seed Pesto 118
Rooty Toot Soup 51

Salad, Beetroot, Caramelised Goat's Cheese and Pumpkin Seed 14
Salad, Carrot, Avocado and Wakame 16
Salad, Chickpea and Quinoa 28
Salad, Green Bean with Lemon and Parmesan 19
Salad, Jen's Broccoli 20
Salad, Nectarine, Pink Peppercorn and Mint Tabbouleh 27
Salad, New Potato and Smoked Mackerel 34
Salad, Puy Lentil, Pea and Mint 31
Salad, Raul's Catalan Artichokes with Aioli 24
Salad, Red Cabbage, Celeriac, Apple and Hazelnut 22
Salad, Som Tam 36
Salad, Summer Chickpea and Tuna 32
Salsa, Peanut with Thai Yellow Curry 114
Sauce, Sweet Red Pepper with Pumpkin and Filo Parcels 86
Sauce, Tomato with Spinach and Ricotta Gnocchi 92
Sauce, Yellow Pepper with Lentil and Sweet Potato Burgers 96
Savoury Pastry 132
Seafood Chowder 68
Smoked Mackerel and New Potato Salad 34
Som Tam 36
Soup, Chorizo and Bean with Kale 76
Soup, Gazpacho 41
Soup, Leek, Sweet Potato and Spelt 46
Soup, Rooty Toot 51
Soup, Spinach 44
Soup, Spring Minestrone 42
Soup, Thai Pumpkin 49
Spelt, Leek, Sweet Potato Soup 46
Spicy Lentils with Grilled Halloumi Cheese 112
Spicy Wedges with Fish in Pakora Batter 58
Spinach and Ricotta Gnocchi with Tomato Sauce 92
Spinach Soup 44
Spinach, Sweet Potato and Comté Tart 130
Spring Minestrone Soup 42
Spring Vegetable Pasta 88
Stew, Catalan Fish 71
Stew, Vegetable and Borlotti Bean 98
Stock, Fish 72
Strawberry and Mascarpone Tart 146
Summer Chickpea and Tuna Salad 32
Summer Fruit Jam 162
Summer Vegetable Pilaf with Yoghurt Sauce 100

Summer Vegetables, Cassoulet of 102
Suquet de Peix 71
Sweet and Sour, Thai Mackerel 56
Sweet Pastry 164
Sweet Potato and Lentil Burgers with Yellow Pepper Sauce 96
Sweet Potato, Leek and Spelt Soup 46
Sweet Potato, Spinach and Comté Tart 130
Sweet Red Pepper Sauce with Pumpkin and Filo Parcels 86

Tabbouleh, Nectarine, Pink Peppercorn and Mint 27
Tagine, Moroccan Fish 64
Tahini and Lemon Sauce with Falafel Burgers 94
Tart, Courgette, Tomato, Basil and Mozzarella 122
Tart, French Apple 150
Tart, Lime and Coconut 153
Tart, Pissaladière 126
Tart, Potato and Chorizo 78
Tart, Roasted Beetroot, Rainbow Chard and Chèvre 128
Tart, Spinach, Sweet Potato and Comté 130
Tart, Strawberry and Mascarpone 146
Tarte au Chocolat 158
Thai Pumpkin Soup 49
Thai Sweet and Sour Mackerel 56
Thai Yellow Curry with Peanut Salsa 114
Tomato and Mozzarella with Linguine 90
Tomato Sauce with Spinach and Ricotta Gnocchi 92
Tomato and Courgette, Basil and Mozzarella Tart 122
Tomatoes and Basil with Grilled Cod 61
Tuna and Chickpea Summer Salad 32

Vegetable Pilaf with Yoghurt Sauce 100
Vegetable Stew, Borlotti Bean and 98
Vegetables, Cassoulet of Summer 102
Vegetarian Moussaka 116

Wakame, Carrot, and Avocado Salad 16
Whiskey Mayonnaise with Grilled Prawns 63
White Wine, Peaches Poached in 142

Yellow Pepper Sauce with Lentil and Sweet Potato Burgers 96
Yellow Thai Curry with Peanut Salsa 114
Yoghurt Sauce with Summer Vegetable Pilaf 100

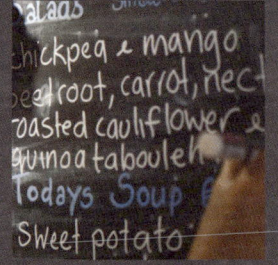